A Companion to Reading Newman's Grammar of Assent

by

Richard Geraghty

En Route Books and Media, LLC
5705 Rhodes Avenue
St. Louis, MO 63109

Cover credit: TJ Burdick

LCCN: 2018960329

Copyright © 2018 Richard Geraghty
All rights reserved.

ISBN-13: 978-1-7325949-8-2
ISBN-10: 1-7325949-8-8

Table of Contents

Foreword 1

Introduction 3

Chapter 1: The Sermon used as an Introduction to the *Essay* 5

Chapter 2: Modes of Holding Propositions 39

Chapter 3: Apprehension, the Third Term (Ch. 1 of the *Essay*) 57

Chapter 4: Assent Considered as Apprehensive (Ch. 2 of the *Essay*) 67

Chapter 5: An Interlude - Philosophical Idealism versus Philosophical Realism 77

Chapter 6: Apprehension of Propositions (Ch. 3 of the *Essay*) 97

Chapter 7: Notional and Real Assent (Ch. 4 of the *Essay*) 111

Chapter 8: Notional and Real Assent (Second Part of Chapter Four of the *Essay*) 127

Chapter 9: Assent and Apprehension in the Matter of Religion (Ch. 5 of the *Essay*) About the Author 145

Chapter 10: Assent Considered as Unconditional (Ch. 6 of the *Essay*) About the Author 161

Chapter 11: Certitude (Ch. Seven of the *Essay*) 173

Chapter 12: Formal, Informal, and Natural Inference
  (Ch. 8 of the *Essay*) 203

Chapter 13: The Illative Sense
  (Ch. 9 of the *Essay*).. 217

Chapter 14: Assent and Inference in Religious Matters
  (Ch. 10 of the *Essay*)..237

Chapter 15: The Truth of Revelation
  (Ch. 10 of the *Essay*).. 247

Afterword 261

Foreword

Blessed John Henry Cardinal Newman is considered by many to have been the greatest apologist for the Catholic faith of the 19th Century. A convert from the Anglican Church, he wrote many books, the most famous of which are probably his Sermons, his autobiographical *Apologia Pro Vita Sua,* and the *Development of Christian Doctrine.*

But one of his best books, *An Essay in Aid of a Grammar of Assent,* is less often read. Even though the arguments in it for why we should believe the truths of the Gospels in spite of the doubts often raised by skeptics are compelling, they require a philosophical acumen not often found even among educated Catholics.

Now, here is Dr. Richard Geraghty with the remedy. As a professor of philosophy for many decades, teaching seminarians, Geraghty has been rated the most popular of teachers because of his gift not only of simplifying difficult concepts, but also of expounding them with brilliance and humor.

In this book, *A Companion to Reading Newman's Grammar of Assent,* Geraghty explains Newman's truths by illustrating them as they pertain to contemporary Catholic issues. In his personal notes, he provides delightful windows into his own soul with its struggles from childhood faith, to confusion, to militant buoyant faith.

If you struggle with doubt this is the book for you. If you are a 100% believer, it will be great to use with doubters you know. Their name is legion.

   -- Dr. Ronda Chervin, *professor emerita, Holy Apostles College & Seminary, Cromwell, CT*

Introduction

The purpose of this book is to take Catholics who have graduated from college or who are in the process of doing so step-by-step through the argument of Blessed John Henry Newman's *An Essay in Aid of a Grammar of Assent*. This classic published in 1870 was written to prepare Catholics for living in the modern age, an age he predicted would be an apocalypse isolating the Catholic Church from the culture in a way she had never experienced before in her long history. Not only that. The age would be well on its way to isolating the culture from its roots in Western Civilization, roots that go back to the great heritage of ancient Greece and Rome. To prepare Catholics for this catastrophe, Newman constructed a philosophical argument of over three hundred and fifty pages. Graduates would be most in need of rehabilitating their imaginations and intellects because the images and notions generated in higher learning would have a corrosive effect on the traditions of both the Catholic Church and Western Civilization.

After long philosophical preparation, Newman's conclusion at the end of the book is quite simple. It may surprise you. It is that to be a sheep in the flock, the Catholic Church, is the best use of reason there is. By "reason," he does not mean only the kind exhibited by such great theologians and philosophers like St. Augustine or St. Thomas Aquinas. He means the kind exhibited by ordinary Catholics. Their witness on this earth is that of a whole body—the laity as well as the hierarchy, the poor as well as the rich, the illiterate as well as the literate, the child as well as the adult. If the flock says its prayers, confesses its sins, offers the Sacrifice of the Mass, and follows the Pope as the Vicar of Christ on earth, it will be more than a match for the Devil and his cohorts in any age. It will be the Church Militant battling its way through this life so that it might be the Church Triumphant in the next.

My message is the same as Newman's. On the leading page of the Grammar of Assent he quotes St. Ambrose: *Non in dialecticâ complacuit Deo salvum facere populum suum*. (It is not by philosophy that God proposes to save his people). How does God propose to save his people? It is by faith, not in Christianity in general, which is a rather vague notion, but in the Catholic Church, which is a definite flock, institution, society, or thing existing now as the Church Militant. There has been from her beginning in the First Century a war with the world that has continued to this day and will last to the end of time. While the educated have their special role to play, it is still that of good sheep saying that higher education is not everything. What is everything is The Faith, the essential characteristic of the Church.

Chapter One

The Sermon Used as an Introduction to the *Essay*

Newman begins the *Essay* without giving a general introduction. Instead, he plunges right in with a definition of terms as if he were just a dried out grammarian or logician. But he is a lot more than that. He is building the foundations of a philosophical argument that will justify belief in the teachings of the Catholic Church. There are, of course, many other ways to spread the truth about the Church. Newman is marking off a philosophical way. It is not an easy one. But who said higher education is easy? Fortunately, however, Newman preaches a sermon three years after he wrote the *Essay* in 1870 entitled "The Infidelity of the Future,"[1] predicting that the modern age will be an apocalypse. The sermon gives us a clear picture of what an apocalypse is. Seeing it will get us ready for studying the *Essay*.

Spread throughout my analysis of Newman's sermon will be

---

[1] John Henry Newman, *Reason For Faith,* Source Books, Box 794, Trabuco Canyon, CA. 92678. Originally published in 1957 as *The Catholic Sermons of Cardinal Newman.* Page numbers will be included in the text. The sermon in slightly different form may also be found by doing a Google search for the Newman Reader.

my comments as an eighty-five year old who lived for about thirty-five in the pre-Vatican Two Church and is still alive today in the wreckage of the Church and the Nation.[2] These comments are not the result of research done in a library but of what I have experienced. So I will not be overly concerned with defending my comments but will simply lay them out for whatever they are worth.

1) What the Catholic Church Is

The sermon is an example of the Church in action. The occasion is that of a priest rejoicing with his people at the inauguration of a seminary for the education of priests. Both preacher and congregation share a common life as members of the same flock; they are believers. In the background are over three hundred years of persecution waged by a government determined to rip Catholicism out from the hearts of the English people where it had been planted by St. Augustine of Canterbury in the Sixth Century. England had been known as Our Lady's Dowry. The Crown has made her the archenemy.

By the year of 1850, the government relaxes because it has pretty well succeeded in stamping out the faith, the remnant being a few Old Catholic families and the mass of Irish Catholic immigrants pouring into big cities like Birmingham to make a living and raise a family. Having won, the government can afford to tolerate the reestablishment of the Catholic hierarchy that had been wiped out by King Henry VIII in the Sixteenth Century. Newman and his fellow Catholics, a despised minority, rejoice that they will be allowed to come above ground again. They can educate their

---

[2] Editor's Note: This book was completed in June, 2017, and Dr. Richard Geraghty died in July, 2017.

priests without fear that they will be hunted down as traitors to the Crown worthy of being hanged, drawn, and quartered, a grisly practice of King Henry VIII continued by his daughter Queen Elizabeth I, known by Anglophiles as Good Queen Bess, the Virgin Queen, and by the Irish under other names. The last execution was that of the Irish priest St. Oliver Plunkett in 1681.

Comment

Being a Catholic has never been easy in any age, but particularly in the English-speaking world since the Sixteenth Century. My parents, having come from the West of Ireland to New York City in the 1930's, knew that. The memory of Oliver Cromwell rampaging through their land in the Seventeenth Century with his army was still fresh in their minds. They came with little money and a grade school education. But they had The Faith. The Blessed Mother and her Son were more real to them than the neighbors next door. My parents knew that the Protestant strain in American culture was no friend of theirs. So they and the immigrants before them supported under the guidance of the Bishops a Catholic educational system to preserve and pass on The Faith and to raise their standard of living. To a system ranging from grammar school to college they contributed their own dimes and their own children to the enterprise. The schools were staffed mostly by priests and religious who worked for practically nothing, thus allowing for a private school system independent of the public schools financed by the tax dollars of the state. While Catholics paid their taxes, they supported their own schools. Due to these efforts, my generation born in the 1930's took for granted that Catholics were finally taking their proper place in America. We were Catholics and Americans on the rise. I happened to be one who left home at the age of fourteen to become a member of a teaching order of brothers and priests. It wasn't as if I became a Catholic due to the books and arguments I read in college. I was stamped long before.

The Question

Back to the sermon: Newman raises the question: What is the purpose of a seminary? While his answer is more sophisticated, it is essentially what I learned as a kid in catechism:

> This handing on of the truth from generation to generation is obviously the direct reason for the institution of seminaries for the education of the clergy. Christianity is one religious idea. Superhuman in its origin, it differs from all other religions. As man differs from bird, quadruped or reptile, so does Christianity differ from the superstitions, heresies, and philosophies which are around us. It has a theology and an ethical system of its own. This is its indestructible idea. How are we to secure and perpetuate in this world that gift from above? (p. 118)

Here we have very strong language indeed. The "Christianity" to which he is referring is not the generic term we use today to cover both Catholic and Protestant beliefs. The term refers to the beliefs of the One and Only Holy Roman Catholic Church. She alone is one religious idea or entity founded by God and differing from all denominations and other religions "as man differs from bird, quadruped or reptile." The Church is God's idea translated into time and place, an actual flock founded for all nations and continents on the globe.

The Sermon Used as an Introduction to the *Essay*

Mere Human Beings

The question arises of how Newman and his people, mere human beings, are to secure and support the divine gift from above. The answer is not vague. It starts with boots on the ground instruction given by priests to families. It is the Catholic Way I learned as a kid in the 1930's and early 40's under the nuns who had us memorizing the Baltimore Catechism. Newman explains:

> The divine provision is as follows. Each circle of Christians has its own priest, who is the representative of the divine idea to that circle in its theological and ethical aspects. He teaches his people, he catechizes their children, bringing them one and all into that form of doctrine, which is his own. But the Church is made up of many such circles. How are we to secure that they all speak one and the same doctrine? and that, the doctrine of the Apostles? Thus: by the rule that their respective priests should in their turn all be taught from one and the same center, viz. their common Father, the Bishop of the diocese. (p. 119)

The doctrine taught above is Catholic. It is by being in the Church as part of the flock that we learn The Faith. We are not just individuals who have chosen to be members of a religious group. Through baptism, we have been inserted into an already divinely constituted society. We have had no choice in the matter. Why should we? Doesn't God have the right to choose the way He will save us sinners? At the grass roots are families taught by a priest. The priest in turn is taught by his Bishop, a descendant of the Apostles. The Bishops in each diocese throughout the world are in union with the Pope, the Bishop of Rome.

The Pope teaches what the Apostles learned from Christ Himself after living three years with him. They learned what is real. Christ has shown Himself to be the Son of Joseph and Mary, the One who will be crucified and raised from the dead. Christ knows this from personal experience because He is the Second Person in union with the Father, the First Person of the Holy Trinity. Thus, He is the only one who has the authority to translate the Word into human institutions and language. He does so for his Apostles. They believe Him. They preach their belief to the rest of the world. The result is the Church as she is today with the authority of Prophet, Priest, and King over all nations and empires to the end of time. That's what I and my generation learned as kids in grade school. Clearly the Catholic Church is making the claim that God Himself in the person of Christ has entered human history and will remain there through his presence of the Church as a society both in this life as the Church Militant and in the next as the Church Triumphant. The Catholic Faith embodies what has happened in the past, is happening now, and will continue to happen for all eternity!

The Big Picture

The above is the big picture the Church impressed upon me and my generation born and raised in the 1930's. We were the inheritors of a battle started in the Sixteenth Century among baptized Catholics. While about two thirds of them remained faithful to the Church, about one third protested against her, thus giving birth to the Protestant version of Christians also embodied in institutions. Hilaire Belloc argues that if King Henry the Eighth had not made himself Head of the Church in Great Britain, the Protestant Revolt would have failed. Although King Henry abhorred the Lutherans and Calvinists on the continent and wished to preserve many elements of the Catholic tradition, he still substituted himself for the Pope, thus making himself a schismatic rather than a heretic. His successors, however, put the Church of England on the road to heresy and apostasy. Those who disagreed with the Crown went to America. When the colonists declared their independence of Great Britain in 1776, they were mostly Protestants. When the United States eventually became a superpower supplanting Great Britain, being a Christian and being a Protestant became equivalent as far as American opinion was concerned. By and large Protestants considered themselves to be the only Christians worthy of the name. There was the strong feeling among many of them that Catholicism with its pope and prelates were superstitious idol worshipers destined for hell if they did not repent! Such is the religious culture in which Catholics immigrants found themselves. Since this culture in the Nineteenth Century was well on the way to becoming totally secular, Catholics also had to deal with an atmosphere of religious indifference.

An Objection

Cradle Catholics are accused of being made so without their consent. Would it not be more fitting, the objection goes, for us to choose our beliefs later on when we have grown up? Would we not thereby show that we are not slavish souls going along on the path laid down by our parents and ancestors obeying prelates? This objection comes naturally from those who are imbued with the Protestant spirit reinforced by the American spirit of political independence.

Yet it is a plain fact of nature that fathers and mothers have conceived us. Half our chromosomes are from the mother and the other half from the father. Much of who we are is them. Still deeper, without their care we would not have survived either physically or emotionally. We are stamped with our parents' beliefs. Even in the natural order we are not as independent of the past as we might like to think we are.

The supernatural order follows the same pattern. In the First Century, baptism began with the Apostles. After the first converts, there was infant baptism that continued for sixteen hundred years. So what's wrong with infants becoming Catholics at the baptismal fount? That's the ordinary way that the Church maintains herself. If there were no babies, there would be no human society, let alone a Catholic society.

The explosive growth of the Church in Africa and India is due to couples who convert and have babies. Some of the babies go on to being priests and religious, thus forming a native clergy in a non-Christian culture. The Church grows her own. It's hard to avoid the conclusion that such is the way the Holy Spirit has operated and continues to operate. It's the natural order laying the foundations for the supernatural order. In contrast, Catholics in Europe are contracepting and aborting themselves out of existence. Catholics in America are doing the same thing.

The Interview of Pope Francis

Another objection is that is that the Church is intent on preserving her exclusiveness by insisting upon obedience to the Pope and the Bishops. The Hierarchy holds the line. We follow along like sheep. Consequently, we have been likened to Communists, Fascists, even Muslims. Perhaps the interview[3] given by Pope Francis when he entered into his ponti-

---

[3] The text may be found in a Google search for the interview of Pope Francis by of the editors of *America* magazine entitled "A Heart Open to God" published on Sept. 30, 2013.

ficate will be helpful in understanding the notion that although the Church is a very definite society, she is an open one. "Here comes everybody!" as James Joyce once noted.

When asked about the way the Pope saw himself, he answered: "I am a sinner." He was only echoing the prayer "Holy Mary, Mother of God, pray for us sinners now and at the hour of our death." All that aspirants and members have to do is to confess their sins and seek Mary's intercession with her Son if they wish to belong. The only type of people excluded are those who claim to be sinless. Who might they be? People who cheat the poor, abort the baby, corrupt the innocent, and do what they damn well please because they have the power. They exclude themselves. But if they wish to be included, all they have to do is admit that they are sinners with the intention of repenting. Then they become sheep in the flock of Christ, the most inclusive society there is.

Accordingly, the Church is a house with open doors, a castle with the drawbridge down. Out of her come big-hearted men and women to live with the masses being crushed by the powers-that-be. They fight the proud and console the afflicted so that the humble may be brought to safety and joy, not just in the next life, but in this life as well. It's a matter of heart speaking to heart so as to include anyone who has not hardened it.

Am I preaching? You bet I am! We should have a clear idea of who we are. It is because of our belief in the doctrines of the Church that we reach out to the world to bring it happiness both in this life and especially in the next. Without belief in the doctrines, we are mere social workers or humanitarians trying to wrest the world from the grip of Satan. No mere human being is that strong.

2) What the Great Danger Will Be

Now let us observe Newman predicting in 1873 the difficulties that Catholics will meet that they have never met before. His listeners have had plenty of experience with difficulties. The Old Catholic families have survived centuries of persecution. The Irish immigrants pouring into the cities have the further burden of being at the bottom of society. But the future has something new in store for their descendants.

> ...I think the trials that lie before us are such as would appall and make dizzy even such courageous hearts as St. Athanasius, St. Gregory I, or St. Gregory VII. And they would confess that, *dark as the prospect of their own day was to them severally, ours has a darkness different in kind from any that has been before it.* [my italics]. The special peril of the times before us is the spread of that plague of infidelity, that the Apostles and our Lord Himself has predicted as the worst calamity of the last times of the Church. And at least a shadow, a typical image of the last times is coming over the world. I do not mean to presume to say that this is the last time, but that it has had the evil prerogative of being like the most terrible season, when it is said that the elect themselves will be in danger of falling away. (p. 121)

A Mouthful

Newman is saying a mouthful when speaking of St. Athanasius (d. 373), Pope St. Gregory I (d. 604), and Pope St. Gregory VII (d. 606) being dizzy and appalled at the prospect of the modern age. The saints had only to deal with pagans and barbarians. Yet they succeeded in shaping society for the better, Christendom being the result. While it was far from perfect (what human arrangement is?), you could see the Church having more and more impact on the culture. Then why would the prospect of the modern age appall the great saints? Because it will seem like it was the apocalypse predicted by Christ. Newman is not presuming that he sees the actual apocalypse coming. The modern age will at least be *like* the apocalypse. But if Newman is right, that's us today. Can our age be that terrible? Newman says it will be. Why? *Because in the past the pagans and barbarians shared some first principles with the missionaries. The modern age will share none of them.*

Lower Than Pagans

Moderns are lower than Pagans such as Socrates, Plato, and Aristotle. The ancients viewed life on this earth as a battle between the just and the unjust. The unjust adopt, not the reality, but the appearance of justice. The just adopt the reality. The result? Socrates is executed by the powers-that-be for being an atheist and corrupting the young. Nevertheless, the ancient trio argued on the basis of reason that the just were still happier than their opposites. The actual experience of their lives told them so. Although they were executed or exiled, they fought the good fight. They died in the expectation that the gods whom they served in this life would stand by them in the next.

Building on this assessment of man's situation on earth as a battle, the Apostles came to Rome preaching that God Himself had become a baby in the womb of the Virgin Mother in order that he might be crucified by the powers-that-be. As usual, the very best is treated as the very worst. But the vindication of the executed does not remain just a hope as it had been with Socrates in his last discussion with his friends. On the third day, after all, Christ rises from the dead. Pagans who preserved their belief that the Immortal

Gods ruled over the affairs of Mortal Men would welcome the news that God had become a man to prove that justice itself was worth pursuing for its own sake. Later on, missionaries to the pagans and the barbarians could appeal to a sense of higher powers ruling the world. There is belief, though often mixed with superstition. In the modern world, however, belief in a divine order will be considered abnormal, unnatural, a relic of a pre-scientific past marked by superstition, idolatry, and abysmal ignorance. It is to this kind of culture that priests and their flock will have to witness in the modern age.

The Cause

Newman asks what is the philosophical cause of the overt infidelity that will plague the modern world. But before we consider the philosophical cause, let us consider the ultimate cause. It is the war begun in the beginning when God created from nothing the universe with intelligent creatures—angels and men—at the top. Lucifer, the Light Bearer, is among the most intelligent. He knows without any doubt that God has created him from nothing. Yet Scripture relates his reaction: "I will not serve." There is a great mystery here. In knowing he is intelligent, he knows he is like God. Accordingly, he has two choices. He can thank God for being like Him, acknowledging he is finitely intelligent and God is infinitely so, which is the plain truth. Or he can resent the fact that he is under the authority of God. He chooses to resent. While he is not stupid enough to think he can defeat God, he will seek to spite Him until the end of time. God allows him the time. But on the final day Satan and his helpers will be confined to hell for all eternity. The Devil already knows that! There is indeed something very mysterious and frightening in this account of revelation. Believers conclude that there are extremely intelligent spirits roaming about the world rejoicing in the violation of the innocent, the crushing of the helpless, the desecration of the sacred. They love it!

The case of our First Parents is only a little less mysterious but still quite so. Adam and Eve are not mere babes in the Garden knowing nothing from nothing. They are in charge of it. Adam has named all the plants and animals in it. He has put the right name on things. A rock is a rock, a plant a plant, an animal an animal and a man a man. He has named his wife Eve, who is bone of his bone, flesh of his flesh. Together they will generate the human race. In the cool of the evening they talk with the Master of the Universe. They are on easy terms with Him and with each other. They are naked to each other and to God.

At first, Eve refutes the lie of the Serpent, pointing out that God did not forbid them all the fruit in the garden, just the fruit of a particular tree. But then she shifts her attention to the fruit, which gleams so brightly and looks so good to eat. She eats and then offers some to Adam. He eats; and the history of the human race enters a new phase. We all have the choice of being creatures grateful to God or rebels who want to be gods ourselves. This war will become more open in an apocalyptic age.

In the early stages of man's history, infidelity to God is more covert because religion has a respected if not always deeply practiced place in society. Unbelievers had to be hypocrites in order to be successful. In the modern age, unbelief will be overt. As far as appearances are concerned, the powers of unbelief will be seen as quite respectable, natural, normal. Here the cool and objective use of language in philosophy will serve as a good cover for diabolical malice, often without philosophers being aware of it. If the Devil can quote the Scriptures, he can fashion syllogisms. Modern thinkers have gotten rid of the awful spectacle of an angelic power taking joy in the attempt to destroy every single thing that the Creator loves. The picture is too barbaric for civilized sensibilities. Instead, we have the more urbane discourse of philosophers trying to enlighten the masses, us.

The Elementary Proposition

What is the elementary proposition of modern philosophers? Newman tells us:

> The elementary proposition of this new philosophy which is now so threatening is this--that in all things we must go by reason, in nothing by faith, that things are known and are to be received so far as they can be proved. Its advocates say, all other knowledge has proof—why should religion be an exception? And the mode of proof is to advance from what we know to what we do not know, from sensible and tangible facts to sound conclusions. (p. 123)

How very reasonable it sounds! Does not our education tell us that we should be reasonable, especially in religious matters? It's as if being religious puts us in imminent danger of being fanatics, lunatics—or worse.

Newman continues to lay out the view of his opponents:

> The world pursued the way of faith as regards physical nature, and what came of it? Why, that till three hundred years ago they believed, because it was the tradition, that the heavenly bodies were fixed in solid crystalline spheres and moved round the earth in twenty four hours. Why should not the method which has done so much in physics, avail also as regards that higher knowledge which the world believed it had gained through

revelation? There is no revelation from above. There is no exercise of faith. Seeing and proving is the only ground for believing. (p. 123)

The reference is to the history of the modern sciences. Until three hundred years ago, men accepted the astronomy of Aristotle until scientists checked out the subject by closer observation. On many points, the scientists were right. Aristotle was displaced. Why should not religion be subjected to the same method of scrutiny? Are not the Middle Ages over and done with? Yet, the Catholic Church still proclaims faith as the truth revealed from above. Thus she claims to be superior to human reason. How can an educated people accept such a strong claim for the value of religious authority embodied in human beings like Popes and Bishops? Should not the educated be able to examine religion in the light of reason? Do not people who have the good fortune to be living in a scientific age have the right to be critical of beliefs held in pre-scientific ages? Is there no such thing as an update, a revision, an accommodation?

Not Obvious

The apocalypse Newman is referring to is not as obvious as the Four Horsemen raining down death and destruction on the earth below. It is more like an odorless and invisible gas breathed in as if it were life-giving air. Who can object to the proposition that religion should be reasonable? And doesn't being reasonable require that the best and the brightest get together to dialogue? In such a setting, prophets are to be thrown overboard for upsetting the crew. If a man-eating whale happens to be swimming by, so much the better. Corpses floating about are bad for the environment.

The Modern Notion of Reason Specifically

More specifically, what is the modern notion of reason? Newman explains:

> They [the philosophers] go on to say, that since proof admits of degrees, a demonstration can hardly be had except in mathematics; we can never have a simple knowledge; truths are only probably such. (p. 123)

Let's unpack this brief description because it is a direct reference to the main topic of the *Essay*. Philosophers, Newman along with them, hold that mathematics allows of strict demonstration. If you understand the demonstration, you are compelled to give your assent to the conclusion. The sheer intelligibility of the proof leaves you no choice. It has to be that a triangle, for instance, has such and such properties. Newman could add that understanding the demonstrations of metaphysics also gives you no choice. Fine! No problem. But what about conclusions concerning an actual state of affair in the world or, to use another term, in concrete matters? For example, what about the claim that England is an island, that Julius Caesar was assassinated in 44 B.C, or that George III was King of Great Britain during the American Revolution? Relatively few of us have been eye-witness to England's island status and none of us to any of the other events. To get the evidence to support these beliefs we have to rely on the testimony of others. But eyewitnesses can be mistaken or even lie. Thus we have to use our power of inferring to check their trustworthiness. In these concrete matters inference does not allow the certitude that comes from demonstrations in mathematics or metaphysics. At best, inference in concrete matters leads only to probabilities.

So where is the conflict between Newman and modern philosophers? It is in this. They conclude that giving assent to the truth of any concrete matter is always illegitimate. If this is so, Catholics are wrong. They give their assent to what they have been taught by priests. The priests say that over two thousand years ago God became a baby in the womb of the Virgin Mary so that He might be crucified, all for the purpose of saving the world from its sins. Need anything more be said about the gullibility of Catholics? On the contrary, Newman concludes that if such assent is given in the right circumstances, it is not only legitimate; it is the way that human beings down through the ages have arrived at certitude not only about religious truths but about moral and secular ones as well. The battle Newman wages against his opponents is carried on in his *An Essay in Aid of a Grammar of Assent. His aim is to provide Catholics who have had the opportunity for higher education with the grammar, the vocabulary, which will enable them to locate through the fog generated by an apocalyptic culture the basic foundations of secular, moral, and religious truths.*

Returning to the Sermon

Returning to the sermon: Newman amplifies the objections of his opponents.

> . . . faith is a mistake in two ways. First, because it usurps the place of reason, and secondly, because it implies an absolute *assent* [italics mine] to doctrines, and is dogmatic, which absolute assent is irrational. (p. 123)

Consequently, it is no surprise that modern thinkers are outraged at the ways of the Church. She teaches what has happened, is happening now, and will happen in the future. Standing as individuals before the judgment seat of God, we will go to our eternal reward or eternal punishment. That's how barbaric the Catholic Church is! Consequently, moderns conclude that the Church sins against reason in two ways. First of all, she substitutes faith for reason. Instead of teaching people how to think, she lays upon them doctrines and dogmas they must hold as definite truths, not as opinions or probabilities. Secondly, she goes to the length of demanding absolute assent to the dogmas she preaches. She calls it a sin against faith for Catholics to say otherwise, a sin can land one in hell if it is not repented of and forgiven. Is she not a thoroughgoing tyrant of thought control in an age when men are liberating themselves from the superstitions of the past?

Newman continues:

> ...you will find, certainly in the future, nay more, *even now, even now,* [italics his] that the writers and thinkers of the day do not even believe there is a God. They do not believe either the object--a God personal, a providence, and a moral governor; and secondly, what they do believe, viz., that there is some first cause or other, they do not believe with faith, absolutely, but as a probability. (p. 123)

Why is Newman so shocked that even in his own day there are thinkers who do not believe in a personal God who watches over mankind? It is because in the 1870's the British still considered themselves to be a Christian nation. While they were differing among themselves about what a Christian is, they would be shocked to hear that some of their eminent intellectuals did not even believe in a personal God.

Summary

From the account given above we can see that Newman has a

very difficult job ahead of him. The difficulty is not just intellectual, a matter for argument. It is in the imagination, the faculty which registers most directly our experience of life. And what is the experience of a true Catholic in the modern world? It is that of a flock or society telling the rest of the world that everybody should repent of their sins in order to avoid the pains of hell and to gain the joys of heaven. How utterly basic the message is! Many are apt to take offense, saying "How can anyone with even a shred of human dignity accept such a message especially when the messengers are sinners themselves? Does it make any sense that sinners have to confess their sins to other sinners like Popes, Bishops and priests?" Consequently Newman as a philosopher cannot deal with his subject matter as if his readers were just intellects calmly and judiciously weighting arguments. He is dealing with human beings who already have strong feelings about what their lives are all about.

Taking into account the story in the Scriptures about Lucifer and our first parents, the basic question about life is this: Who is God? Is it Him or is it Me? All of us have the tendency to say it is "Me". That's the Original Sin. And so the war begins, not just between the City of God and the City of Man, but also within the heart of every human being. For a philosopher not to take into account this egotistical thrust present in all of us (and in himself) is to be unreal. We are not judicious intellects calmly weighing arguments. We have an emotional interest in the outcome. We have skin in the game, a dog in the fight.

A Personal Note

If I had read this sermon in the 1960's, I would have missed the point, feeling that while the past was difficult for my parents and ancestors, the present and future were much brighter for my generation. I had been teaching as a religious brother in various high schools throughout the country since I graduated in 1954. It seemed to me that the Church and the nation had never been in better shape. Catholic education was booming and the nation, having defeated the Godless Axis powers, was facing down the Communists in Soviet Russia. That was my state of mind and that of many other Catholics of my generation. We figured that our fellow Americans would no longer consider it a contradiction that we could be loyal both to the Pope and to America. We had arrived. Or so we thought! The point of the story? Newman saw an apocalypse coming. Over ninety years later, my associates and I were still dreaming of a new and better age when we were actually living in the apocalypse that Newman predicted. Who would have thought that something as humongous as an apocalypse could sneak up on us?

3) Signs of the Coming Apocalypse

In the second part of his sermon, Newman gives examples from his own time which have led him to the conclusion that an apocalypse is coming upon his England and, eventually, upon the modern world. In the following he answers an objection.

> You will say that their theories [those of modern philosophers] have been in the world and are no new thing. No. Individuals have put them forth, but they have not been currant and popular ideas. Christianity has never had experience of a world simply irreligious. Perhaps China will be an exception. We do not know enough about it to speak but consider what the Roman and Greek world was when Christianity appeared. *It was full of superstition, not infidelity.* (my italics) (p. 124)

The Sermon Used as an Introduction to the *Essay*

To make this kind of judgment you have to know history. He goes on to say that between the Apostles and their pagan listeners there were first principles held in common; namely, that the divine order ruled the affairs of men both in this life and the next. Later, came the northern barbarians who, amid all their superstitions and brutality, were believers in an unseen Providence and in a moral law. As mentioned above, Saints Athanasius, Gregory I, and Gregory VII had their difficulties. Newman's conclusion? "But we are now coming to a time when the world does not acknowledge our first principles."(p. 124). The modern age will be unique in its utter rejection of a divine order.

A Refinement

He refines his use of the term "the world." Just as God revealed to Elias that in the rebellious kingdom of Israel there were seven thousand who had not bent their knee to Baal, so in the time when Protestantism has replaced Catholicism in England, there will be a remnant who belong to the soul of the Church, though their eyes have not been opened to see her as their true mother (p. 125). Yet they will still share first principles with Catholics. He is not referring to them. Who is he referring to?

> But I speak first of the educated world, scientific, literary, political, professional, artistic—and next of the mass of town population, the two great classes on which the fortunes of England are turning: the thinking, speaking and acting England. My brethren, you are coming into a world, if present appearances do not deceive, such as priests never came into before, so far as you go beyond your flocks, and so far as these flocks may be in great danger as under the influence of the prevailing epidemic. (p. 125)

Newman goes on to specify the difficulties that priests and their people will meet. First is that the form of Christianity embraced by the nation will be in decline.

> Most of them [the Christian Churches], nearly all of them, already give signs of the pestilence having appeared among them. And then as time goes on, when there will be a crisis and a turning point with each of them, then it will be found that, instead of their position being in any sense a defense for us, it will be found in possession of the enemy. (p. 126)

We have seen in our time what Newman saw in his; namely the breakdown of Protestant Christianity. In 1928, the Church of England was the first Christian denomination to break nineteen hundred years of tradition and allow artificial contraception for married people. Other groups followed. Then the issue of abortion came along. Later came the issue of homosexuality (sodomy), same sex marriage, euthanasia, transgenderism, and the rest. How long the Baptists down here in the American South will resist the pressure is hard to say. The majority of Catholics in the Northeast where I come from have already collapsed. It is the home of liberal Catholics, those who have been quite successful financially due to their education by the nuns and brothers. How ironic!

Another Difficulty

He notes another difficulty. It is plain that "we are at the mercy of even one unworthy member or false brother." The newspapers will pick up the story and spread it all over the land. Catholics are already great objects of malicious curiosity. "If there ever was a time when one priest will be a spectacle to men and angels it is in the age now opening upon us." (p. 129) There is no need to amplify on this point.

The Sermon Used as an Introduction to the *Essay*

Just say the words "child molestation," "priestly celibacy," and "cover ups," and we have an open and shut case against the Church as far as the public is concerned.

Three Years Ago

I wrote the paragraph above about three years ago when it was not yet clear to me that that there had been a cover up by many Bishops for the sexual misbehavior of their priests. The secular press can be a bit biased, to say the least. Today (January 12, 2016), it is becoming public that the Archdiocese of New York, to cite one of many other cases, has been under the increasing influence of a homosexual clerical clique that specializes in cover-ups. The scandal has begun to be noted by the secular press and is bound to stay in the news because it includes violations of criminal, civil, and ecclesiastical law. The courts will be involved for all the world to see in daily dispatches.

I used to think that the Catholic Church was immune to these kinds of evils because we had a Pope and the Protestants didn't. But the Pope (in this case Pope Francis) is having difficulties with many Cardinals and Bishops who insist in word and deed that couples who are divorced and remarried should be able to receive Holy Communion. They further insist that the homosexually inclined bring special gifts to the Church. They conclude that such acts should not be condemned as intrinsically evil. In most cases Catholic academia agrees with them, not the Pope. At the same time, the majority of the lay folk re-elected Barack Obama as President. I find this situation hard to believe. Nevertheless, a fact is a fact. If readers wish to know more about it, they can tune into Michael Voris at his web site Church Militant, as I do, a fact that may shock some my friends who are as orthodox as I am. Michael is not "nice".

So, why bring up such disturbing matters when my intention is to take you through a long and leisurely analysis of *An Essay in Aid of a Grammar of Assent*? It's because I am certain that such an analysis has a place in a time when we are beginning to see and feel what an apocalypse is.

The great catechist Fr. Hardon, S.J., was asked the question of how Judas fit into Christ's plan. Did he not work miracles and drive out devils like the other eleven? Father's answer was that Judas was an example that even divinely appointed bishops and priests can end up in hell. What bigger apocalypse can there be?

I bring this matter up because it touches on the great mystery of evil. It has to be that Christ knew absolutely everything before He founded the Church. And yet he still placed his Bride in the hands of men. It has to be that He knew what He was doing. The question for us Catholics today is whether we believe it. The psalms at Mass have us singing "Alleluia, the battle is won!" It is. But we need faith to sing it with any enthusiasm.

Mysteries

Back to Newman: Still another difficulty will arise from the fact that the teachings of the Church are mysteries. Explaining and defending them will be difficult in an age that is unsympathetic to treating even the mysteries of nature with respect, let alone those of religion. He explains:

> And hence the popular antipathy to Catholicism seems, and will seem more and more, to be based on reason, or common sense, so that the charge will seem to all classes of men true that that the Church stifles the reason of man, and next that, since it is impossible for educated men, such as her priests, to believe what is so opposite to

reason, they must be hypocrites professing what in their hearts they reject. (p. 130).

Newman was often accused of being a hypocrite because his detractors thought him too intelligent to be a real Catholic, thereby consigning the rest of us to being either fools, fanatics, or morons, take your pick.

A Personal Note

Only in the 1980's did I realize what the apocalypse was that Newman predicted. In the twenty years preceding that realization, I went through different stages. When the 1960's began, I was a teaching brother in a religious order dedicated to Catholic education in the same way that the older brothers had been. We took for granted there was a fit between our loyalty as Catholics to the Pope and our pride in being Americans.

When the Council of Vatican II closed in 1965, I and my generation were euphoric for what was called "The Spirit of Vatican II". It appeared that the Church was ready to leave her confinement and enter fully into the mainstream of national affairs. But soon after I was confused by the fact that my order, which had been noted for its family spirit, was being torn apart by dissension. For that to happen among a band of brothers is heart breaking. On the one hand there were those like myself who held that our mission to the world could still be carried on by men in communities wearing habits and teaching the catechism as well as the various arts and sciences. On the other hand were those who considered that such devotion to the schools was pandering to the tastes of the middle class. They wanted to break out of this mold and reach out to the desperately poor by becoming community organizers, lawyers, or doctors. They would not wear habits or live in large communities. They would take a social worker's approach to the role of spreading the Gospel.

The dissension that followed saw the departure of unprecedented numbers of brother and priests from the order, thus leaving the schools understaffed, a mere shell of what they used to be. The home I had chosen as a fourteen year old was collapsing around me. But I was too preoccupied to pay much attention to large events. For example, in 1967 the Presidents of about ten leading Catholic colleges and universities got together and signed the Land O' Lakes document stating their resolve to remove their institutions from the supervision of the Bishops and place them under lay boards. In 1969, Catholic theologians publicly dissented from the encyclical of Pope Paul VI *Humanae Vitae* upholding the traditional view of marriage and condemning artificial contraception. In 1973, the Supreme Court of the United States decreed that abortion was a constitutional right. I had not yet put two and two together on any of these issues because, as I said, I was more concerned the collapse of my religious congregation than with larger events.

In 1972, at my request the superiors gave me permission to take up doctoral studies, hoping that I would choose a doctorate in psychology as a most practical and useful endeavor suitable for modern times. Instead, I chose to study the likes of Aristotle and St. Thomas Aquinas because I had been taught they embodied unchanging truths. Catholic academics were backing off that claim, suggesting that Catholics should pay more attention to modern philosophers. Bothered by this suggestion, I wanted to check the matter out for myself. Either those truths had been demonstrated or they hadn't. I was going to get to the bottom of it. So off I went with permission to reside at a university outside the community and live more on my own. I suppose

The Sermon Used as an Introduction to the *Essay*

there was also the motive to escape the pain of seeing my fellow brothers at enmity with each other—and with me.

Having gotten my degree, I then started looking for a position in a Catholic college or university. In the old days, Thomistic philosophy teachers were as plentiful as buffalo feeding on the Great Plains. Catholic institutions required of their graduates a large dose of Catholic theology and philosophy no matter what their specialties. But Catholic institutions had changed because of their desire to compete with the more prestigious secular institutions and to get more government money. Their rise in society led them to sell out their heritage. They were filled with the "Spirit of Vatican II". I found myself in the painful position of being a buffalo with no habitat. The spirit of the times had hit home. It got my attention the way a two-by-four gets the attention of a jackass who has been whacked over the head.

To put an even sharper point on it, I realized that a brother trained to live in community does not do very well in resisting the world, the flesh, and the devil when living more on his own. My ventures were not as lurid as those of St. Augustine. But having more time on my hands and being my own superior, I was free to explore modern culture in the movies and novels it produced. They were filled with images either of ecstatic lovers riding off into the sunset or of tragic lovers suffering the pangs of unrequited love. In contrast, ordinary marriage with Ma, Pa, and the kids seemed dull, routine, middle class, stilted or whatever. So did living as a brother in a regular community. My daydreams did not lead to overt action but they sure made saying my prayers, going to confession, and attending mass less frequent and fervent than they should have been. Masturbating does not help one's prayer life.

Around the same time, I renewed my habit of reading Newman's sermons. As usual, Newman's quiet but persistent way renewed the Fear of the Lord in me. When he quietly puts you before God as the creature you are, you realize that a fine gentleman like myself can end up in hell. You have the appearance of being pure and chaste but not the reality. Pressured by such thoughts within and difficulties without, I resolved to start flying a lot straighter. Going to confession became part of my routine again.

In that frame of mind, I turned to some unfinished business. When the controversies began in the late 60's about the Pope's condemnation of artificial contraception, I was surprised about the opposition of the American Theological Society to it. Wasn't the Pope the Vicar of Christ on Earth? Nevertheless, I did not take sides. I would let the higher ups deal with the matter. I was a brother, not a priest who heard confessions. Nor was I a husband with a wife. So in teaching Catholic moral philosophy, I did not say anything about what seemed a disputed question.

Looking back on this decision, I see it as a wedge placed between my belief that the Pope is the Vicar of Christ on earth and the teaching that artificial contraception is an intrinsic evil. There were an insightful few who saw the connection, but I was not one of them. And so I left the matter to be decided by the higher-ups. Being a teacher of moral philosophy, I should have known better. But I didn't.

After about twenty years of indecision on this particular point, it was time for me to take another look. I remember taking a book off the shelf written by Pope John Paul II (now Saint John Paul II) twenty-five years after Pope Paul VI condemned artificial contraception. John Paul II had not changed this teaching one bit. He spoke as if the theologians for the last twenty-five years had never existed. So I had to choose between the Pope and the theologians. Having enough Fear of the Lord left in me, I chose the Pope although there were still many things I did not understand about the issue. It was as simple as that! But simple decisions can take a long time in coming. Having taken that stand, however, I was pleasantly surprised to discover in a short while that all the philosophical texts I had learned fell into line. I could finally see the nature of marriage by the use of reason. But it was a use of reason preceded by a reawakened faith. It was actually true that sticking to the faith led to understanding. Yet great numbers of theologians far more intellectually gifted than I continued to say very clever but really very stupid things.

In 1988, I left my order about the age of fifty-seven. I resolved not to live under its banner anymore because I had lost faith in my superiors. I then got a position as a layman teaching Thomistic philosophy in a Catholic seminary. To my happy surprise, they wanted someone like me.

During that period, I got married. I had not left the order for that purpose. But after feeling the loneliness, I started looking for a wife. I soon found out, however, that I would be doing myself and the intended no favors because I was far from being a domestic type. But the women my age I dated were supremely domestic. I then figured on remaining single, reconciled to go on teaching the college seminarians. And then Rebecca Halonan came along. Making one of the best moves I ever made, I married her. Although born and raised an atheist, she had been hanging around with some Catholic friends who took her to Mass. Impressed by the fact that I was teaching in a seminary, she would ask me questions. The result was that she became a Catholic, thus making it possible for us to have a Nuptial Mass.

But then the Cardinal replaced the administration that had hired me with a new one more according to his liking. By this time, I was not surprised at the "don't ask, don't tell" attitude" of the majority of Bishops and of the priests towards artificial contraception. This attitude introduced a terrible contradiction into the lives of both clergy and laypeople. The Popes continued to call the act an "intrinsic evil" while the many if not most of the priests and lay people continued to act as if the whole matter was simply a matter of individual conscience. I had seen that the unspoken permission to make the use of The Pill, an oral contraceptive supposedly legitimate for married people, opened up doors to all sorts of new theories about the nature of marriage and even the nature of man and woman. Finally, digesting that bitter fact, I made a special point of teaching the evils of contraception. But I was in for another surprise.

I discovered a permissive attitude in the seminary towards ordaining men with homosexual inclinations. I recall a discussion we had with a priest who had come down from the Chancery. He spoke in glowing terms of being open to whomever God had provided. I asked him whether I would be branded a "homophobe" if I rejected the idea that having homosexual inclinations was permissible for candidates to the priesthood. He did not answer the question. But I could see that I would have a new memo in my dossier. Not only would I be a pre-Vatican II Catholic and an opponent of artificial contraception. I would also be a "homophobe," a hater of men.

It's a wonder I lasted nine more years teaching in that institution. During that time, I got to know men who wanted to be priests and had homosexual inclinations. One had already been sexually abused by a Bishop no less. I suppose that the administration figured it would be easier to bear with me rather that to kick me out. But there is such a thing as "death-by-administration." Sooner or later, the administration gets its way by being patient and legal, above all by being legal. They build up a file showing how you have defied the "reasonable" requests of rectors and faculty senates—and then they spring the trap. After nine years, I figured my time was coming to a close. I resigned. There was a nice dinner where I was given gifts to speed me on my way. So off I went to teach at another place that was far more orthodox. I was to teach at the House of Studies on the Eternal Word Television Network founded by Mother Angelica. And that's where I am at the time of this writing. (By the way, she just died on Easter Sunday at the age of 93.)

Looking Back

Looking back at what I have written, I have noticed that I did not say anything about the changes in the celebration of the Mass that were made after Vatican II. Since I had been an altar boy, I knew in detail what those changes were in the Latin Mass. Until the age of thirty-three, I knew of no other way to have the Mass celebrated. While I regretted the loss of Gregorian Chant in the changes, I was not particularly disturbed by the other changes. It was only about thirty years later that I realized how destructive of true religion those changes were. No longer a religious brother, I happened to attend a celebration of the Latin Mass with my wife. The congregation was waiting quietly in their pews when the bell rang and out of the sacristy four altar boys in cassock and surplice came, followed by the priest. While the congregation knelt, the priest faced the altar and immediately began to say the prayers at the foot of the altar to which the servers responded with their set prayers. There were no greetings, exhortations or other preliminaries by a presider—just the serious business of repenting sinners being led to offer sacrifice. Later on, as the priest elevated the Host, bells were rung and the altar boys placed their hands at the bottom of the chasuble and raised it as if to free the arms of the priest so that he could raise the Host and then the Chalice. I well-remembered the gestures because I had done them hundreds of times as an altar boy. Although I was not particularly well read in liturgical matters, I immediately saw the tremendous difference between repenting sinners worshipping Christ and the so-called People of God offering bread and wine by means of a presider. While the liturgists has taken care to inform us that the bread was still the Body of Christ and the wine still His Blood, they had changed the gestures as if they were interchangeable. But anyone with eyes to see and ears to hear could tell they were not interchangeable. They imparted different messages. The old message had been put aside so that it seemed as if the Tridentine Mass allowed by the Pope had been restricted by the Bishops, surely an odd situation. Could it be that the smoke of Satan has entered into the sanctuary, which was question uttered in dismay by Pope Paul the Sixth? The example shows that an apocalypse can be a very sneaky thing. It can creep up on even those who still go to Mass, a number much less than 50 or 60 years ago. But to say so is not seen as very nice by many Bishops.

At The Eternal Word Television Network (EWTN), I have found that the popular devotions I had known as a youth are still alive and well. Ordinary people held on to them like good sheep while we the educated have often wandered in confusion. Here was Mother Angelica, a nun in the Poor Clares with a high school diploma, founding a global network, something neither the Bishops nor the universities were able to do. Miracles, both physical and spiritual, actually happened here. At any rate, my wife died in 2012, God rest her soul. She was a good woman who showed me the joys of married love. At the time of this writing, I am alone working on my Newman book.

When I began writing this book about fifteen years ago, I wondered whether there would be any young people wanting to read it. I was still reeling from the shock of the Church falling apart in my own times. But recently like an old buffalo out in the dry plains I have been sniffing the coming of a rainy season. I have taught young adults, often reverts or converts, who have been eager to take their places in the flock, which is a lot more resilient than I thought it was. The Holy Spirit is still hovering over us with those great wings of his—but it sure doesn't look that way. We need faith to get beneath the pain and feel the joy.

4) Newman's Answer to the Coming Apocalypse

What is Newman's answer to the coming apocalypse? Is it to be found in educated priests and laity mastering the types of argument found, for example, in such works as the *Essay*? Will his advice be that Catholics attend to their intellectual development to prepare themselves for the types of controversy that will inevitably ensue in a culture dominated by unbelief? No! Consider the answer he gives in the very last paragraph of his sermon.

> This [a sound knowledge of their religion], though it is not controversial, is the best weapon (after a good life) in controversy. Any child, well instructed in the catechism, is, without intending it, a real missioner. And why? Because the world is full of doubtings and uncertainty, and of inconsistent doctrine—a clear consistent idea of revealed truth, on the contrary, cannot be found outside the Catholic Church. Consistency, completeness, is a persuasive argument for a system being true. Certainly if

> it be inconsistent, it is not truth. (p. 133)

Thus ends the sermon! Obviously, Newman is not requiring that all Catholics go to college. Rather he is calling for a renewal of faith in the Church. What is the Church? She is the unique Christ-founded flock that has been baptized, catechized, and forgiven so that all men and women of good will might see God face-to-face in the eternal kingdom. Hence, even a child who has been instructed in the catechism and lives a good life will be a successful missionary.

Conclusion

The purpose of this chapter has been to prepare us for reading the *Grammar of Assent*. We will do so as Catholics conscious of being Catholics. If we are in higher education, we will get no points for that profession. But that's their problem, not ours. When push comes to shove, why should we be ashamed about being a sheep in the flock of Christ? We are believers. That is our glory and salvation.

In fact, Catholics don't even have to be able to read and write. Many down through the ages have not been literate. But they had something more essential; namely, the identity of being sheep in a flock that will endure and even flourish despite the efforts of emperors, kings, presidents and devils either to seduce or to crush her. She is protected even from the infidelity of an Apostle named Judas Iscariot, heretics like Father Martin Luther, or couples that contracept. For she has been entrusted to the Holy Spirit by Christ. The powers of hell will not prevail against her. They will not prevail against any of us who unite with our fellow sheep in proclaiming that the Devil does not run the world. We do so because of the fact that we are willing to follow our Master in being murdered like Him—and then rise from the dead.

Chapter Two

Modes of Holding Propositions (Chapter One of the *Essay*)

There is logic behind our profession of The Faith. Concerning such events like God's being born a baby of the Blessed Virgin Mary in a stable in Bethlehem over two thousand years ago, we believe they happened because God has told us so through His Church. Since God cannot be wrong, we are eminently logical in holding that these events happened. Now, it is obvious that those who don't believe reject this logic. The result is the great divide separating believers and unbelievers. We believers stand ready to die for the truth, thus imitating Our Master. There will be a time, however, when all debate will cease. That will be on Judgment Day when Christ decides the whole matter in person. There will be no more doubt, difficulty, or confusion.

But on this side of the grave there is another way besides faith in the Church to learn the truth about what actually happened. It is by way of a practical philosophy. But it is a long and difficult way to follow that requires special training. It is this way that Newman proposes in *An Essay in Aid of a Grammar of Assent.* In this work, he will put over his vestments as a priest the robes of a philosopher. His starting point will be the self-evident truth that we humans are bodies with sense knowledge of other bodies like rocks, trees, animals, or men. His goal will be to show after over three hundred pages of argument that the best use of reason, a faculty that all humans possess by the fact that they are human, results in belief in the Church.

The Text

The very first paragraph of Chapter One goes as follows:

Propositions (consisting of a subject and a predicate united by the copula) may take a categorical, conditional or interrogative form.

1. An interrogative, when they ask a Question, (e. g. Does Free-trade benefit the poorer classes?) and imply the possibility of an affirmative or negative resolution of it.

2. A conditional, when they express a Conclusion (e.g. Free-trade does therefore benefit the poorer classes), and at once imply, and imply their dependence on, other propositions.

3. A categorical, when they simply make an Assertion (e.g. Free-trade does benefit), and imply the absence of any condition or reservation of any kind, looking neither before nor behind, as resting in themselves, being intrinsically complete. (p.9)[4]

There is nothing more basic than the fact that human beings

---

[4] *An Essay in Aid of a Grammar of Assent* by John Henry Newman, edited with introduction and notes by I. T. Ker, Clarendon Press, Oxford, 1985, p. 9. The pages of the texts quoted will be included in the text.

express their knowledge of the world and of themselves in propositions. What exactly is a proposition? It consists in words which connect a predicate with a subject by means of a copula. Many examples could be used to illustrate this point. Newman picks one from the field of economics. We may say that Free-trade[5] is such that it benefits the poor; or we may say that Free-trade is such that it does not benefit the poor. Thus there arises the question of whether we should affirm or deny the predicate of benefiting the poor with the subject of Free-trade. This type of proposition is interrogative.

The second type of proposition follows naturally from the first type because it is the effort to answer a question. It is a conclusion drawn from premises. For example: Free-trade therefore benefits the poor. The term "therefore" indicates that the truth of the conclusion depends upon or is conditioned by the truth of the premises. If the premises are true, then the conclusion will be true. If the premises are false, the conclusion will be false. In either case we hold the conclusion in a conditional way.

The Syllogism

The syllogism provides a good example showing why all inferences (conclusions) are held conditionally.

> Whatever makes the production of goods cheaper (Middle term) benefits the poor. (Predicate)
>
> Free-trade (Subject) makes the production of goods cheaper. (Middle term)

---

[5] Free-trade is the practice of nations trading their goods without putting tariffs on them.

Therefore Free-trade (Subject) benefits the poor. (Predicate)

Symbolically expressed, there is the following: if M is P and S is M, therefore S must be P. If it true that whatever makes the production of goods cheaper benefits the poor, and Free-trade makes the production of goods cheaper, it follows necessarily that Free-trade benefits the poor. The truth of the first two propositions, the premises, has to be shown by giving evidence drawn from economic realities. A syllogism, then, shows the factors involved when men look for an answer that has been prompted by a question. They respond by inferring or reasoning from premises to a conclusion, the conclusions being held conditionally, meaning on condition that the premises are true.

The Next Type

The next type is the categorical, declarative, or assertive proposition: e.g. Free-trade benefits the poor. No qualifier like "therefore" is attached. No reference is made to premises. Its form indicates that the speaker intends to state an unqualified or unconditional truth. We assume that the speaker is a serious person who, having devoted a great deal of effort to reasoning about the effects of Free-trade, has already reached a conditional conclusion. But now he has gone one step further. Without referring to any premises he takes the personal stand of starting without any qualification or condition that Free-trade benefits the poorer classes. In doing so, he is not necessarily right. But neither is he necessarily wrong. Whether he is right or wrong depends on whether his statement is in accord with the facts.

More Specific

Newman is not content laying out these abstractions. He gets more specific, saying:

> The internal act of holding propositions is for the most part analogous to the external act of enunciating them; as there are three ways of enunciating, so are there three ways of holding them, each corresponding to each. These three mental acts are Doubt, Inference, and Assent. A question is the expression of a doubt; a conclusion is the expression of an act of inference; and an assertion is the expression of an act of assent. To doubt, for instance, is not to see one's way to hold that Free-trade is or that it is not a benefit; to infer, is to hold on sufficient grounds that Free-trade may, must, or should be a benefit; to assent to the proposition, is to hold that Free-trade is a benefit. (p. 10)

Newman argues in the way that accords with common sense. He starts with the physical facts, which are spoken words or written symbols. The facts are in the public domain. He then reasons back to the internal states of mind that caused them so that they too will have public recognition. He is reasoning from the effects (spoken words or written symbols) back to their causes, our minds. By means of our minds we grasp what things in the world are essentially. For example, we say "This is a dog and that is a man." Reflecting on the words, we have the images of a particular dog and a particular man in our minds. The dog is essentially an animal and the man is essentially a rational animal. Notions or ideas are predicated of particular things. We can ask the question "What is a dog or a man?" The sentence expresses a doubt. Finding an answer, we say, "Therefore this dog is an animal and that man is a rational animal." We have a conditional proposition. We may then go on to say without any qualification "This dog is an animal and that man is a rational animal." We have an unqualified proposition, an assent.

There is a similarity or analogy between the external act of enunciating propositions and the internal act of holding them. The form of a question is a result of a mind in doubt. Can the predicate of benefiting the poor be affirmed or not of the subject Free-trade? The form of a conclusion (Therefore Free-trade benefits the poor) is the result of the mind having performed the act of inferring or reasoning. The result is a conditional hold on a proposition. If such and such premises are true, it follows that the conclusion is true. Finally is the form of a flat assertion or categorical statement: Free-trade benefits the poor. There are no conditions or qualifiers attached. There is no argument included in the form of the proposition. We may assume that some type of reasoning has been involved. Reasonable people don't go around making such statements without having thought about them to some extent. An assent is the result of a mind holding a proposition to what it takes to be an unqualified truth. It is a personal adherence to the truth of a proposition without the attempt to offer an argument in its favor. We are not necessarily right in doing so. Nor are we necessarily wrong. We are simply acting according to our nature as rational animals.

Pause For a Moment

Let us pause for a moment. In laying out the definitions Newman is following in the footsteps of the ancient pagan Greek Aristotle whom Newman acknowledges as his secular master (p. 277). But even if we know hardly anything about Aristotle, we do have our common sense. That sense tells us that when we humans face the world, we have ourselves on one side and physical bodies like rocks, plants, animals, and men on the other. In our effort to understand them, we speak to others and to ourselves. In doing so, we use sentences or propositions. If we take the time to analyze this experience, we will come to the same conclusions as Aristotle does. He is simply reflecting on what all of us do naturally. He considers what human beings do and then explains it with precision. In doing so, he solidifies his identity as a rational animal. Newman will do the same for us.

Pause Again

Let us pause again to get a firmer hold on the three types of propositions. The interrogative is clear. We wonder whether a predicate is either to be affirmed or denied of a subject. The conditional is also clear. A conclusion following upon stated premises is true on condition that the premises are true. Included within the conclusion is a term like "therefore". An assent is also clear. Propositions like "God exists" or "Great Britain is an island" include no reference to premises. They are in the form of straight-out assertions. But the reasoning that has preceded these assents is quite different. The assent "God exists" may be preceded either by a philosophical demonstration or by the faith of a child. The assent "Great Britain is an island" may be preceded by having direct knowledge of the fact or by believing in the report of eyewitnesses. Nevertheless, the propositions themselves are in the form of assents, not inferences.

Note

Note that the exposition so far has not required the use of special instruments requiring a great deal of money or government grants. Everybody has the facts to be analyzed because everybody asks questions, infers conclusions, and goes on to make assertions. Further, everybody has the natural wit to organize or analyze these facts, the result being definitions, propositions which are the same for all human beings in all places at all times. The result is a body of knowledge which meets the high standard of being a general science above all the lesser sciences like mathematics, biology, physics, and the rest. It is philosophy pioneered by the ancient Greeks. It was considered the highest of the sciences because it dealt with what was most fundamental. I still subscribe to that view.

The Next Step

The next step is so obvious that we may wonder why Newman bothers to take it. He says:

> Moreover, propositions, while they are the material of these three enunciations, are the objects of the three corresponding mental acts; and as without a proposition, there cannot be a question, conclusion, or assertion, so without a proposition there is nothing to doubt about, nothing to infer, nothing to assent to. *Mental acts of whatever kind presuppose their objects.* [my italics] (p 10)

The key statement is: Mental acts of whatever kind presuppose their objects. How more obvious can he be? If there were no propositions in the mind, there would be no questions, conclusions or assents. For they exist only in a mind. Fine! But why does Newman bother to make such an obvious claim? What's his point? The answer turns on the interpretation of the term "object". It is obvious that the term applies to ideas in the mind like questions, conclusions, and assertions. But these notions existing in the mind come from sense experience of individual things existing in the world. Common sense tells us that our acts of questioning, inferring and assenting have for their goal the knowledge of things in the world. Consequently the ultimate objects of our knowledge of the world are not ideas, notions, or definitions.

Rather they are the truth about individual things existing in the world. Ideas or definitions are the means by which we understand individual things essentially.

Things, actions, or events exist on their own whether we aware of them or not. When we know them, it is because we see, smell, hear or touch them as animals do. We do not have to prove they exist. Unlike other animals, however, we have the ability to know them under the general notion of "bodies". We now have our first principle; namely, there are bodies existing in the world. This proposition does not need proof. It is self-evident. It is first. In the very act of saying it, we understand it to be true. Further, we do not have to acknowledge this principle in so many words. Its truth is implicit in more specific propositions like "There are rocks, plants, animals, or men in the world" or "Free-trade is an economic fact". There is an identity between us and things in themselves when we know them. The identity is not perfect. Initially, all we know is that they exist. We are certain of it. But we need more experience of life to get a better idea of what they are.

Similarly, Newman observes people asking questions, making inferences, and assenting. We do this to express our knowledge of the world in which we live. Under many different circumstances we do this in either speech or writing. Newman disregards the circumstances, which vary indefinitely, and zeros in on the essential nature of these activities. Whether people are children or adults, uneducated or educated, poor or rich, a question is a question, an inference an inference, and an assent an assent. These activities have each their own nature, essence, or identity. They also have relations to each other. A question leads to inferring or reasoning for the purpose of reaching a conditional conclusion that may or may not be held as an assent, is always unconditional.

A Philosophical Realist

At this point Newman is intent upon laying out the key terms of his argument in the manner of philosophical realist, thus taking for granted that man has experience of individual bodies allowing him to define the kinds of bodies there are. At this point of the argument, however, you will have to take my word for it that Newman is preparing an attack on philosophical idealists, his opponents. The chief of them is René Descartes (1596-1650), the Father of Modern Philosophy. Starting his philosophy by casting doubt on the existence of bodies in the world, the Frenchman takes for granted that he has only images and ideas of bodies in his mind, not knowledge of bodies as they exist in the world. His reasoning is that since man becomes aware of bodies in the world through his senses, he has the images and definitions of bodies in his mind. Quite right! But rather than taking for granted the causal connection between the contents in his mind with the bodies outside of it, he chooses to doubt it. In contrast, Newman takes for granted that our experience of individuals asking questions, inferring conclusions conditionally, and assenting unconditionally enables us to define these activities in general. As a philosophical realist, Newman finds this process to be quite natural. It is our experience as individuals who know the facts that entitle us to define them. Descartes casts doubt on the connection between the things of experience and our definitions. Thus, we have the distinction between philosophical idealists and philosophical realists. A realist holds that a definition gives us the nature or essence of the individual thing in question. An idealist holds that a definition is merely an idea in the mind, not an insight into the nature or essence of an individual body in the world.

There is a huge difference between these two stands. To start with things in the world is to have an objective standard to be used in judging the truth of the images and notions we have in our minds. The question of whether, for example, there is a tree in my yard or not is settled by whether it is actually there or not. If we take a look and see it is there, we have the truth. Case closed. Those who say otherwise are wrong. But if we start just with images or notions in the mind, we lose this objective standard, thus leaving us at the mercy of the way different individuals happen to see things. It is to be entirely subjective.

Keeping this difference in the back of our minds will make us more aware of the mental therapy that Newman will put us through. I am assuming that because of our education we have been affected to one degree or other with the mental disease of philosophical idealism. Thus, we are all in need of Newman's therapy.

Three Types of Character

Newman now fills in with more detail the three states of mind expressed in interrogative, conditional, and categorical propositions; namely, a mind in doubt, a mind inferring, and a mind assenting. He says:

> And in fact, these three modes of entertaining propositions,—doubting them, inferring them, assenting to them, are so distinct in their action, that, when they are severally carried out into the intellectual habits of an individual, they become the principles and notes of three distinct states or characters of mind. For instance, in the case of Revealed Religion, according as one or other of these is paramount within him, a man is a sceptic as regards it; or a philosopher, thinking it more or less

> probable considered as a conclusion of reason; or he has an unhesitating faith in it, and is recognized as a believer. If he simply disbelieves, or dissents, then he is assenting to the contradictory of the thesis, viz. to the proposition that there is no Revelation. (p. 10-11)

Newman fills in the notions of doubt, inference, and assent with the three types of characters they produce when judging matters of revealed religion. There are people who are uncertain about whether the claims of revealed religion are true or not. They have questions and are looking for answers. Then there are people who answer that these claims are more or less probable due to their reasoning about it. They are the philosophers, those holding their conclusions conditionally. Finally, there are the believers, those who hold their beliefs unconditionally. They have unhesitating faith in revealed religion. Opposed to them are unbelievers rejecting the claims of revealed religion. They are the dissenters opposing the assent of believers. In opposition to the proposition that there is divine revelation is the contradictory assent there is no divine revelation.

In this brief paragraph, Newman reveals the role he will be taking in his *Essay*. He will be speaking as a philosopher using his ability to reason to conclusions in the concrete order about the truth of divine revelation. His conclusions admittedly will be only conditional, probable. But the man taking on this role will already have given his unconditional assent to the truth of divine revelation. He is a Catholic. The question is this: Will he be able to convince us by the use of reason alone, which admittedly leads only to conditional or probable conclusions in concrete matters, that we can become absolutely certain that the Catholic Church has been founded by Christ over two thousand years ago? Can it be that a Catholic is capable of reaching such a conclusion as a philosopher?

So Far

So far Newman has been setting up his definitions drawn from ordinary experience. There should be no reasonable objections to them. Nevertheless, he hints at some objecttions.

> Lastly it cannot be denied that *these three acts [doubting, inferring and assenting] are all natural to the mind*; [my italics] I mean, that, in exercising them, we are not violating the laws of our nature, as if they were in themselves an extravagance or weakness, but are acting according to it, according to its legitimate constitution. (p. 11)

Newman claims that the three acts are natural to us. We do them as instinctively as fish swim or birds fly. He hints that some philosophers consider this claim to be a violation of reason, an act of extravagance, and a weakness.

Newman answers:

> Undoubtedly it is possible, it is common, in the particular case, to err in the exercise of Doubt, of Inference and of Assent; that is, [1] we may be withholding judgment about propositions on which we have the means of coming to some definite conclusion; or [2] we may be assenting to propositions which we ought to receive only on the credit of their premises, [3] or again to keep ourselves in suspense about; (p. 11)

He is quite thorough in listing the various mistakes we can make. We can ask the wrong questions, draw the wrong conclusions, or give our assent when we should withhold it. While the purpose of these three acts is to get the truth about the state of the world, these acts often result in error.

Continuing, Newman answers that

> ... such errors of the individual belong to the individual, not to his nature, and cannot avail to forfeit for him his natural right, *under proper circumstances*, [my italics], to doubt, or to infer, or to assent. We do but fulfill our nature in doubting, inferring and assenting; and our duty is, not to abstain from the exercise of any function of our nature but to do what is in itself right rightly. (p. 11)

We ask questions, draw conclusions, and give our unconditional assent to what we hold to be definitely true. But what we hold to be true is not necessarily true. We may have made a mistake. But it may also turn out that we have not been mistaken. We may have gotten it right. How will we be able to tell the difference? We already know that man of his very nature asks questions, reasons to conclusions, and gives his assent. To determine whether he is right or wrong in a particular case, we cannot jump to the conclusion that he is automatically wrong. He is just following his nature as a rational animal. Nor can we jump to the conclusion that he is automatically right. We are prone to error. To draw a conclusion one way or the other, we have to consider the evidence. We must get down on the deck, so to speak, and consider more closely the particular circumstances in which we infer and assent.

Conclusion

Newman concludes as follows:

> So far in general:—in this *Essay* I treat of propositions only in their bearing upon *concrete matter* [my italics]

Modes of Holding Propositions

and I am mainly concerned with Assent; with Inference, in its relation to Assent, and only such inference as is not demonstration... (pp. 11-12)

Let me expand on what he means by "concrete matters". They deal with propositions like Great Britain being an island, Julius Caesar having been assassinated, or Henry the Eight having been the King of England. The direct way to get these particular kinds of truths is to be an eyewitness. Eyewitnesses do not have to reason or infer their way to the truth. They experience it directly! Since, however, most of us have not been eyewitnesses to the island status of Great Britain and none of us to historical events back in the past, we have had to rely on eyewitnesses to get the truth. But eyewitnesses can tell the truth, be mistaken, or even lie. Therefore, we have to use our power of inference to discover those whose word can be trusted. But here even the best use of inference leads only to conclusions that are just highly probable. We can question one who purports to be an eyewitness all day long without getting the absolute proofs provided in geometry. For example, just by looking at a triangle we can demonstrate with impeccable logic that all triangles have the property of interior angles adding up to 180 degrees. The conclusion is not a mere high probability; it is an absolute certainty.

We have seen two types of inference which are of their nature conditional because their conclusions depend on premises. There is demonstrative inference characteristic of sciences like geometry or metaphysics. Here the conclusions are absolutely true. And there is inference used in concrete matters like the trustworthiness of eyewitnesses. At best, the conclusions here are only highly probable, never absolutely certain in themselves. Newman's opponents conclude that giving unconditional assent to any proposition dealing with concrete matter is illegitimate. Newman concludes that giving unconditional assent to the truth of a concrete matter is not only legitimate, but it is also the normal way we acquire certitude about the truth of such matters.

So Far

So far, Newman has been laying down the foundations of his argument by putting its key elements in place like a conscientious workman. At this point, we do not know the details of what he will build on these foundations. But we do know that whatever he builds on them has to fit the foundations exactly. Having been informed about exactly what those foundations are, we are now in a position to judge what he builds upon them. Eventually, we will see that the building is the Holy Roman Catholic Church as the embodiment of truth. Can Newman show by the use of reason alone that my parents from the West of Ireland were absolutely right in being Catholics? Can he show me that I have been right in following them? Can he show you by the use of reason alone that you have been right in being a cradle Catholic or a convert? These are the questions.

Step of the Argument

Since we are concerned with the structure of the argument, I will end each chapter with a brief summary of what has transpired structurally. Basing himself on the facts supplied by ordinary experience, Newman maintains that in concrete matters we hold the conclusion of an inference conditionally and then may or may not go on to give unconditional assent to its truth. In the case of such matters as the island status of Great Britain or the fact that Moscow is a city in Russia, we give unconditional assent to their truth even though we have never been there. These facts are proofs against theories that say otherwise. We are, however, a long way off from justifying the proposition that giving assent to the truth of religious matters is legitimate. But we have made a good start by rejecting the theory of modern philosophers that such assent is always illegitimate.

Chapter Three

Apprehension, the Third Term (Chapter One of the *Essay*)

If Newman had continued his line of investigation, he would have answered the objection of his opponents that the conditional nature of inference rules out the legitimacy of unconditional assent to the truth of any concrete matter. But checking The Table of Contents, we see that he defers his answer to Part II entitled "Assent and Inference". He now switches the direction of his investigation by proceeding to define the third term of his argument—apprehension. He will stay on this topic for the rest of part I entitled "Assent and Apprehension," (Part I). Get a copy of the book and check The Table of Contents. We are not analyzing the Grammar of Assent 101. We are analyzing the Grammar itself. Settle down for a long read.

As Usual

As usual, he starts his explanation of apprehension with a lesson in logic. We hold the inference "Therefore x is z" as the conclusion of a syllogism. If x is y and y is z, therefore x must be z. (p. 12) The inference makes sense because it follows from premises. In contrast, the assent "x is z" stands alone. It is an unconditional proposition. But we don't apprehend the meaning of the predicate. Therefore, we do not apprehend the meaning of the subject. This proposition is inapprehensible. Let us now see the weight that Newman puts on this point of logic:

> By our apprehension of propositions I mean our imposition of a sense on the terms on which they are composed. Now what do the terms of a proposition, the subject and the predicate, stand for? Sometimes they stand for certain ideas existing in our own minds, and for nothing outside of them; sometimes for things simply external to us, brought home to us through the experience and information we have of them. All things in the external world are unit and individual, and are nothing else: but the mind not only contemplates those unit realities, as they exist, but has the gift, by an act of creation, of bringing before it abstractions and generalizations, which have no existence, no counterpart out of it. (p. 12-13)

Newman makes a sharp division between images or ideas in the mind and things outside of it. Things in the world are unit, individual. They are bodies that exist on their own whether we know them or not. When they are known, they are known first through sense experience. The results are images of individual things in our imaginations. There is an obvious difference, then, between things existing in the world and the images of them. There is also a similarity. The images in the imagination re-present the bodies in the world. To the reality of a cat sitting on a fence we have the image of a cat sitting on a fence. Animals have this ability to have images of things because they have senses. Humans have this ability plus the further ability to organize these images of bodies into various kinds of bodies. Thus we have the ideas or notions of rock, tree, animal, or man in general. We don't have to be deep in philosophy to recognize the difference between individual things in the world and our images or ideas of them. The difference is a matter of ordinary experience. Nor do we have to be philosophers to recognize the difference between the image of a thing, a particular, and our idea or notion of the kind of thing it is. We say easily enough "This cat on the fence is an animal." Cats can't say that.

More Specific

Newman gets more specific, reminding us again of some basic grammar:

> Now there are propositions, in which one or both of the terms are common nouns, as standing for what is abstract, general, and non-existing, such as "Man is an animal, some men are learned, an Apostle is a creation of Christianity, a line is a length without breadth, to err is human, to forgive, divine." These I shall call notional propositions, and the apprehension with which we infer or assent to them, notional. (p. 13)

The fact that the predicates are common nouns means that they are abstractions or general ideas. They exist only in the mind. But because they have been abstracted or drawn from images which have come from things, notions, or ideas refer to what bodies are essentially. For example, the image of a cat on a fence gives rise to the notion of a cat in general. Thus, we can say that cats are animals. He calls such propositions notional. And the way they are apprehended, which is as abstractions or ideas, is notional apprehension.

He continues:

> And there are other propositions, which are composed of singular nouns, and of which the terms stand for things external to us, unit and individual, as "Philip was the father of Alexander," "the earth goes round the sun," "the Apostles first preached to the Jews." And these I shall call real propositions and their apprehension real. (p. 13)

Again, he speaks in grammatical terms. First are things, unit, individual. Then there is the expression of things in a proposition joining a predicate to a subject. The propositions are about particular things. Thus, our apprehension is real. Note again that man's sensory knowledge of things, of bodies, is the only direct contact man has to the ever changing and steady flow of them in time and place. We do not reason or infer this knowledge. We experience it directly. The more experience we have of things, the more we are able to define them with precision.

The Truths Established

The first truth Newman established was that we hold a proposition either as an inference, which is conditional, or as an assent, which is unconditional. The second was that assent is either notional or real, notional when given to the truth of a notion, real when given to the truth of a thing. These two kinds of truth reflect the status of individual things in the world. Existing in themselves as individuals, things are known by sense knowledge. This knowledge is in images or phantasms from which the intellect draws universal ideas or notions. For example, from images of "this rock," "this tree," "this cat," or "that man," we abstract the ideas of rock, tree, cat, or man in general. Rocks are minerals, trees are plants, cats are animals and men are human beings. We apprehend notions notionally.

Fills in Details

Having laid out his general principles, Newman begins to use them in examining the details of ordinary experience:

> Next I observe, that the same proposition may admit of both these interpretations at once, having a notional sense as used by one man, and a real sense as used by another. (p. 13)

Newman is starting to get personal. Our experience varies with who we are.

> Thus a school boy may perfectly apprehend, and construe with spirit, the poet's words, 'Dum Capitolium scandet cum tacita Virgine Pontifex'; he has seen steep hills, flights of steps, and processions; he knows what enforced silence is; also he knows all about the Pontifex Maximus, and the Vestal Virgins; he has an abstract hold

on every word of the description, yet without the words therefore bringing before him at all the living image which they would light up in the mind of a contemporary of the poet, who had seen the fact described, or of a modern historian who had duly informed himself in the religious phenomena, and by meditation had realized the Roman ceremonial in the Age of Augustus. (p. 13)

It makes a big difference about who is uttering a proposition. A schoolboy and an historian read the same passage from the poet Virgil depicting a Roman ceremony. The object is a real event. Although the schoolboy understands all the words, he does not have real apprehension. In contrast, an historian who has spent his life learning about Roman ceremonies has a sense of the scene close to what a contemporary Roman might have had. The words written by the poet centuries ago put the historian right in the middle of the event. His apprehension is real. The apprehension of the schoolboy is notional. The conclusion to be drawn is that a proposition composed of singular terms is not necessarily apprehended in a real way. The type of apprehension depends on the experience of the observer, a subjective factor involved when assent is given to what is taken to be a truth.

Contrasting Example

Newman then gives contrasting examples of how a notional proposition may be apprehended really.

> Again, 'Dulce et decorum est pro patria mori' [It is fine and noble for one to die for his country] is a mere common-place, a terse expression of abstractions in the mind of the poet himself, if Phillipi is to be the index of his patriotism, whereas it would be the record of experiences, a sovereign drama, a grand aspiration, inflaming the imagination, piercing the heart, of a Wallace or a Tell. (p. 130)

Although this proposition about the glory of dying for one's country is notional, it can be apprehended in a real way. The poet who wrote about the nobility of death on the battlefield is said to have run away at the battle of Phillipi. The truth in his head had not worked itself down to his legs. His assent was only notional. In contrast are the heroes of Scotland and Switzerland for whom the abstraction about giving one's life for his country was also a burning image in their hearts. The point is that notions can be apprehended really. Besides the objective factor of the truth, there is the personal factor in the way of apprehending it. If we have little or no experience in a field, we hold even real propositions notionally. With great experience we hold even notional propositions really. An alligator is the same animal for a zoologist and a layman. But if the layman has nearly been eaten by one, he has real apprehension even though he may not be able to define exactly what an alligator is.

His Method

We have seen enough of Newman in action to get a good idea of the method he is using He will first address himself to our intellects with a few logical distinctions. Then he will illustrate them with examples appealing to our experience of life, an experience which begins with sense knowledge and so impresses our imagination. Despite the fact that we live in a culture which tries to put an overlay of political correctness upon us, we are still human beings with our own powers of sensing and imaging the world around us. While the views that the community takes of what is going on are very powerful because we are social animals, we are still not mere animals. We are rational animals and so are ultimately responsible for our thoughts, words, and deeds. If Newman is right, we have been coated with false images the way that iron can be covered with rust or a ship with barnacles. We must get back to the basic experience we have of ourselves. A baby is indeed a baby, not a blob of flesh. A man and a woman are designed to fit in with each other, not units which just happen to have different plumbing. Newman of course did not have such startling images in mind because he lived in the Victorian age. But that age still had plenty of false overlays of its own. Using his examples, he wants us to scour the rust and scrape off the barnacles so that we will recall our identity as human beings. Once we get more real, we will have given our intellects something real to reflect on. The scouring is necessarily a long process because the distortions laid upon us by living in the modern age have accumulated over time. The atmosphere has been polluted. We have to get back to reality, to the way things actually are in life. It takes a long time to recover from false impressions generated by an elite determined to shape us according to their idea of what a human being is, not according to what a human being actually is. Mental health in the modern atmosphere is not acquired quickly or easily.

Real Apprehension is Stronger

Newman follows up with an observation that is quite obvious.

> Of these two modes of apprehending propositions, notional and real, real is the stronger; I mean by stronger the more vivid and forcible. It is so to be accounted for the very reason that it is concerned with what is real or taken for real; for intellectual ideas cannot compete in effectiveness with the experience of concrete facts. Various proverbs and maxims sanction me in so speaking, such as 'Facts are stubborn things', 'Experientia docet', [Experience teaches], 'Seeing is believing'; and the popular contrast between theory and practice, philosophy and faith. (p. 14)

Like Aristotle or Aquinas, Newman could have gone on to give a metaphysical explanation. Instead, he is content to note the facts as sufficient for his purpose. They speak for themselves. He continues:

> Not that real apprehension, as such, impels to action, any more than notional; but it excites and stimulates the affections and passions, by bringing facts home to them as motive causes. Thus it indirectly brings about what the apprehension of large principles, of general laws, or

of moral obligations, never could effect. (p. 14)

To act is to have made a choice. Real assent conditions our choices because it affects our imagination. Thus, there is always a subjective or emotional factor involved in trying to get a particular truth. Because we each have a body, we take in the things around us with either positive, neutral, or negative emotions. Although we live in the same physical world as others do, we are affected in different ways because our circumstances are unique to us. We live in our own skins, not anybody else's. At the same time we have a mind that enables us to get the general truth about the way the world is in itself. The notion of an orange in general is pretty much the same for everybody. We can communicate easily enough about it. But real apprehension puts us in our own world of particular things. For example, my cousin has a special feeling for oranges—he hates the very sight of them. They were all he ate when he hired himself out to orchard growers for some cash as he was travelling throughout California. Each of us has his own personal experience of things.

The Argument So Far

In his introduction Newman has set up the two main pieces of his argument; namely assent in relation to inference and assent in relation to apprehension. Assent in relation to inference is that of an unconditional to a conditional. Newman's opponents reject this relationship, arguing that the conditional conclusion of an inference requires that the assent be conditional, not unconditional. To accept this view is to negate common sense and the Catholic Faith. Newman will argue against them in Part II entitled "Assent and Inference". In Part I entitled "Assent and Apprehension," he will devote himself to showing the difference between assent to the truth of a notion and assent to the truth of a thing. To accept this view you will be on the way to justify common sense and the Catholic Faith.

He will devote the first five chapters of Part I to the topic of assent and apprehension. The first four will be devoted to matters of ordinary experience and the fifth to matters of religion. It is who we are that determines how we take in the truth of a proposition. If we have a large experience of life, we apprehend the truth in a real way. If we have less experience, we apprehend the truth in a notional way. The young student and the historian are an example. Dealing with the same event of a Roman ceremony, the two have widely different apprehensions. It is this difference that Newman wishes to investigate.

I feel almost apologetic in mincing and dicing our ordinary experience in such abstract terms. But if we wish to be philosophers, we have to be precise in our analysis of our ordinary experience. Our ordinary experience is the result of reasoning that is amazingly complex when you try to analyze it. Just as our experience of hitting a baseball or knitting a sweater requires years of analysis in a lab in order to grasp exactly how these acts can take place, so our experience in sensing and defining things takes centuries of philosophical analysis. The theologians tell us that angels can know things all at once because they have no bodies and hence no senses. Since we have senses, we have to learn about things one step at a time. We have to experience them one by one, day by day.

Step of the Argument

In Chapter One of the *Essay,* Newman has defined the three main terms of the argument—assent, inference, and apprehension. In Chapters Two to Four under the general title of Part I "Assent and Apprehension" he will show that in ordinary matters real assent moves us more powerfully than notional assent because the former makes its appeal to the imagination while the latter makes its appeal to the intellect. In Chapter Five, Newman will apply the lessons learned to religious matters.

Chapter Four

Assent Considered as Apprehensive (Chapter Two of the *Essay*)

Newman will now proceed in Chapter Two to illustrate the all-important concept of real assent with the example of a mother teaching her child. This illustration is of prime importance because it begins at the very beginning when human beings start to live and think. We start within a framework inherited from our parents. Trust in the word of authority is the starting point. We start out in life dependent on our parents not only for our physical existence but also for the way we view the world before we go on to develop our own particular way of looking at it as we get older. Unfortunately, today this bond between parents and children is often broken. But if we are still alive, we have had surrogates. So at the very start we are all *believers*. The apple does not fall far from the tree. Whether the apple turns out to be sound or rotten, our parents or surrogates are a factor. How do we know that? We are still alive, aren't we? Those who took care of us must have done something right!

A Logical Point

After noting the logical point that we have to apprehend the meaning of the predicate before we can assent to the truth of a proposition, Newman says:

> If a child asks, 'What is Lucern?' and is answered, 'Lucern is medicago sativa, of the class Diadelphia and order Decandria'; and henceforth says obediently 'Lucern is medicago sativa, etc.', he makes no act of assent to the proposition which he enunciates, but speaks like a parrot. (p. 17)

The child asserts. He does not assent because he does not apprehend the predicate and so does not apprehend the subject. But the child is not a parrot. It is a human being. Thus, it is able to ask about the meaning of the word "lucern". Newman continues:

> But, if he is told, 'Lucern is food for cattle,' and is shown cows grazing in a meadow, then, though he never saw lucern, and knows nothing at all about it, besides what he has learned from the predicate, he is in a position to make as genuine assent to the proposition 'Lucern is food for cattle' on the word of his informant, as if he ever knew so much more about lucern. And as soon as he has got as far as this, he may go further. He now knows enough about lucern to enable him to apprehend propositions which have lucern for their predicate, should they come before him for assent, as, 'That field is sown with lucern' or 'Clover is not lucern.' (p. 17)

The child already knows from his own experience the difference between food and an animal eating it. Perhaps he has a pet dog. But he does not know the meaning of the word "lucern". He asks his mother. She points to cattle grazing in a field and says that lucern is their food. He accepts the meaning of the word "lucern" on her authority. Since the child already knows the meaning of the predicate "food for cattle," he has a truth about the subject. His assent to the proposition is due to sight. He sees the cattle eating lucern.

Along with the grasp of this particular fact is the generalization that lucern is a type of food that cattle eat. While there is a lot more to lucern than being food for cattle, he knows at least this. From this slight beginning the child can then go on to express further propositions. Having an idea of what lucern is, the child can then use it as a predicate to state other truths. He will be able to say that a field is full of lucern or that clover is not lucern. With more experience he can eventually become a botanist or at least a parent teaching a child. Here we have the unconditional assent to a proposition that is intelligible or apprehensible to him. It is an assent based on knowledge.

A Reflection

The child is a human animal. Therefore, he has been able to learn language from his elders and use it to know the world around him better and thereby learn more about himself. He is his own center of progress, not merely an animal run by instinct. He is what all of us have been and still are. While we are still dependent upon others and always will be, we have a certain independence that animals don't have. We are human beings able to realize our potential to learn by our activity of knowing things.

The Inapprehensible

In the next section, we come to Newman's main concern, which is the nature of belief. He asks whether the child can give assent to a proposition that is entirely inapprehensible (unintelligible) to him. In the previous example, Newman explained how the child gains knowledge that it can then use to gain further knowledge about the world. Now the question is whether the child can attain belief in the truth of a proposition for which he has no apprehension. Newman answers:

> Yet there is a way, in which the child can give *an indirect assent* [my italics] to a proposition, in which he understood neither subject nor predicate. He cannot indeed assent to the proposition itself, but he can assent to its truth. He cannot do more than assert that 'Lucern is medicago sativa,' but he can assent to the proposition 'That lucern is medicago sativa is true.' For here is a predicate which he sufficiently apprehends, what is inapprehensible in the proposition being confined to the subject. (p. 17)

Newman highlights a fact that moderns overlook; namely that belief or trust in the word of authority is a major factor in our understanding of the world in which we live. While the proposition that lucern is medicago sativa is inapprehensible to it, the child can assent to its truth. Why? Because his mother says so. Newman goes on to explain further:

> . . . the child's mother might teach him to repeat a passage of Shakespeare, and when he asked the meaning of a particular line, such as "The quality of mercy is not strained," or "Virtue itself turns vice, being misapplied," she might answer him, that he was too young to understand it yet, but that it had a beautiful meaning, as he would one day know: and he, in faith on her word, might give his assent to such a proposition,—not, that is, to the line itself which he had got by heart, and which would be beyond him, but to its being true, beautiful, and good. (p. 17)

Because of trust in the word of his mother, the child gives his assent to, believes in, a great many things of which he has no apprehension. His real assent to the word of his mother is the prelude to a great many other assents that will provide him with the gateway to the traditions of society, to a reverence for literature and to a love of science. Trust in the word of an authority is the key we use to open the door to our understanding of the world. Without this key, we would be buried in isolated pieces of sense knowledge without a clue to how they fit together. The words of Shakespeare are good. The words of drunks in a brawl are bad. The words in the catechism like "Thou shalt not commit adultery" or "Thou shalt not covet thy neighbor's wife" are good even though the child does not understand what "adultery" or "coveting" means. But he knows those actions are bad.

Yet experience shows that mothers, parents, and teachers may be defective. Trust in their word may lead the child to a warped view of the world. The child may be led to distrust males, to be suspicious of outsiders, or to become antisocial. The result depends upon the character of the authorities who have taught it. Nevertheless, the truth remains that our parents have set the beliefs impressed upon us. We are as not as independent of the views of others as moderns like to think. For better or for worse, we are dependent upon others for our both for our existence and for the beliefs with which we start our lives.

While all assents are in the form unconditional propositions, there is a difference between them. The assent to the proposition "Lucern is food for cattle" is based on the child seeing it. The assent is based on sight. The assent to the proposition "That lucern is medicago sativa is true" is held by the child because it trusts in the word of its mother. The child *believes*. It is the assent due to belief with which Newman is most concerned in his *Essay*. Why? Because he is ultimately concerned with justifying belief in the Catholic Church. But before Newman gets to this religious matter of belief, he explores the matter of ordinary of belief. Since he accepts the saying that grace builds on nature, he will examine nature first and grace later.

A Difference

Newman goes on to show that some authorities carry more emotional weight than others. He says that

> by reason of this circumstance of his apprehension he would not hesitate to say, did his years admit of it, that he would lay down his life in defense of his mother's veracity. On the other hand, he would not make such a profession in the case of the propositions, "Lucern is food for cattle," or "That lucern is medicago sativa is true"; and yet it is clear too, that, if he did assent to these propositions, he would have to die for them also, rather than deny them, when it came to the point, unless he made up his mind to tell a falsehood. That he would have to die for all three propositions severally rather than deny them, shows the absoluteness and completeness of assent in its very nature; that he would not spontaneously challenge so severe a trial out of the two of the three acts of assent, illustrates in what sense one assent may be stronger than another. (p. 18)

When the authority is its mother, the child will fight for the truth of her veracity. While it is just as true that "Lucern is food for cattle" or "That lucern is Medicago Sativa is true, the child will not be inclined to fight about it. He has no skin in the game, no dog in the fight. His mother's honor is different.

Newman explains his methodology:

> I am examining the act of assent itself, not its

> preliminaries, and I have specified three directions, which among others the assent may take, viz. assent immediately to the proposition itself, assent to its truth, and assent both to its truth and to the ground of its being true,--"Lucern is food for cattle,"—"That lucern is medicago sativa is true," --and "My mother's word, that lucern is medicago sativa, and is food for cattle, is the truth." Now in each of these is the one and same adhesion of the mind to the proposition, on the part of the child; he assents to the apprehensible, and to the truth of the inapprehensible and to the veracity of his mother in her assertion of the inapprehensible. (p. 18)

A great deal about life is inapprehensible to the child. Indeed, a great deal of life is inapprehensible to adults. Most of us only believe that $E=MC^2$ on the authority of scientists, not because we understand it. What is most vividly apprehensible to the child is the trustworthiness of its mother. It is this basic trust that affects assent to the truth of other propositions. The starting point is personal. In this encounter, we have the roots of the drive to get the truth about the world around us. There is the belief that the words of Shakespeare, the lessons of science, or the dictates of tradition are true, beautiful, and good. Propelled by real assent to the word of elders, we strive to understand other beliefs as best we can. We believe so that we may eventually understand. It is our belief in the trustworthiness of authorities that stamps us. In this regard, mothers have more power with us than other authorities like dictionaries or teachers.

But there are parents who are not as sound as they should be. Having the wrong beliefs, they instill wrong beliefs in their children. This must have happened quite frequently in the last five hundred years, the evidence for such a claim being that our present age is an apocalypse. It did not come upon us like the bubonic plague, a non-human cause. It came upon us from what had taken root in the hearts and minds of parents engaged knowingly or not in the battle between The City of God and the City of Man.

Real assent or belief is the key to understanding how individuals and communities live their lives. The starting point is the spontaneous trust that children place in the word of their parents. We are all are believers from the very beginning. While we know the truth about matters within our own experience of life like, for instance, lucern being food for cattle, there is still a great deal about life that is inapprehensible to us. We come into an already constituted world as a blank tablet. We are necessarily believers in the authority of our parents and elders because without trust in them or their surrogates we would not have survived. This dependence upon our elders is the natural order. The apple does not fall far from the tree because it comes from the tree in the first place.

Role of Inference

Newman has illustrated the notion of real assent with the example of the child trusting in the word of its mother. Does inference have any role to play in this process? We can rule out the conscious use of the syllogism. We can also rule out the conscious process of informal inference. What remains are the impressions left on the child by the smiles and the soothing words and actions of its mother. Somehow these impressions bring out the trusting response of the child. In one sense he is like a pet dog or cat. At the same time he is more than that. He is a human animal. Somehow the impressions left on him lead him to the conclusion that he is loved and cherished by someone out there in the big world.

He responds accordingly. He believes. Here we have a kind of inference. But it is not the conscious progression of one idea to another but rather the progression of one thing to another. It's a kind of rational instinct seen especially in children. Whom they love or hate is a big factor in how they think, in how we think.

Role of Authority

Newman's example of the mother and child reminds us of the role that authority plays in our existence and, hence, in our thinking. An authority is the author or source of what follows from it. Parents are the authors of babies who in turn grow up to be parents, the result being the continuation of the human race. Our parents obviously have an effect on the way we view the world. Belief in their word is the gateway to all further knowledge of what we take to be true.

Why is Newman being so obvious? It is because he is performing the role of a philosopher. He is taking everybody's experience of having been a baby and showing what is necessarily involved by breaking it down to its essential elements. In theory, there should be no doubt about the results. But as we will see in the next chapter, there has been plenty of doubt in the modern age.

Step of the Argument

Everybody starts out in life trusting in the word of his or her parents and teachers. We are stamped. All of us are *believers* dependent upon others for the way we first view the world. We are not primarily creatures of reasoning or inferring. Rather we do our reasoning *after* we have believed. This is the path that human nature lays out for us. We can either follow its way or try to create another way, as Descartes did. He will be the subject of the next chapter.

Chapter Five

An Interlude: Philosophical Idealism Versus Philosophical Realism

I will now take the liberty of interrupting the flow of Newman's argument for the purpose of highlighting a feature which he develops in later stages. That feature is that he is a philosophical realist preparing us to overcome the infection of philosophical idealism that permeates modern readers—us. Unless we recognize this infection in ourselves, we will not understand what Newman is trying to do for us; namely, to get us over the bad habit of confusing things in the real world with our own notions or images of things. There is a big difference. Without further ado, then, let me do a face-off between a philosophical realist following nature's way and a philosophical idealist rejecting nature's way and following his own.

Descartes lays out his views in a work entitled *Meditations on First Philosophy*. He begins as follows:

> Several years ago now I observed the multitude of errors that I had accepted as true in my earliest years, and the dubiousness of the whole superstructure I had since then reared on them; and the consequent need of making a clean sweep for once I my life, and beginning again from

the very foundations, if I would establish some secure and lasting result in science. But the task appeared enormous, and I put it off till I should reach such a mature age that no increased aptitude for learning anything was likely to follow. Thus I delayed so long that now it would be blameworthy to spend in deliberation what time I have left for action. Today is my chance; I have banished all care from my mind, I have secured for myself peace, I have retired by myself; at length I shall be at leisure to make a clean sweep, in all seriousness and with full freedom, of all my opinions. (p. 61)

He accepted in his early years what everybody else had accepted; namely, that human beings are bodies with sense knowledge of other bodies in the world. Upon the foundations of this fact, the Pagan Aristotle erected the science of metaphysics (first philosophy), the study by the use of reason alone of the physical world to learn what is beyond the physical. The Christian St. Thomas Aquinas followed with a version of first philosophy whose starting point was also found in sense knowledge. But what has been the result of centuries of thought according to Descartes? No certainty! Philosophers are still debating the old questions and reaching contradictory answers. How unlike the scientists of his day who, although divided in their religious beliefs, are making great progress in the study of nature! They are beginning to master it in a way the ancients never dreamed of doing. Consequently, Descartes figures it is time to put philosophy on a new foundation. He considers himself just the man to do it. He has already made significant contributions to science by his mathematical discoveries. He asks why traditional metaphysics cannot be as conclusive? It can be if it uses the right method. He is in no doubt that he has the right method.

An Interlude

He continues:

> To this end I shall not have to show that they [his previous opinions drawn from sense knowledge] are all false, which very likely I could never manage; *but reason already convinces me that I must withhold my assent no less carefully from what is not plain and indubitable that from what is obviously false*; [my italics] so the discovery for some reason for doubt as regards each opinion will justify the rejection of all. This will not mean going over each of them—an unending task; *when the foundation is undermined, the superstructure will collapse of itself;* [my italics] so I will proceed at once to attack the very principles on which all my former beliefs rested. (p. 61)

Descartes is quite aware of the importance of first principles. They dictate the path of the reasoning that follows from them. His method will be the revolutionary approach of withholding his assent from any view about which he can have the least doubt. What is the first principle on which he casts his first doubt? He tells us:

> What I have already accepted as true *par excellence* I have gotten either from the senses or by means of the senses. Now I have sometimes caught the senses deceiving me; *and a wise man never entirely trusts those who have once deceived him.* (my italics) (p. 61-62)

He puts his explosive under the first principle of philosophical realists. He does not deny the existence of the physical world as a practical matter. He would have gone insane if he doubted the existence of the food on his plate or of his companions at the dinner table. Rather, he doubts that the starting point of philosophy consists in the sense knowledge of bodies. He doubts that seeing, hearing, smelling or touching things are sufficient for being certain about their existence. Thus, he doubts even that he has a body! There is nothing natural about the path he is taking. He is being unique, someone special, unlike the rest of men. He is an intellectual fascinated with the clarity of demonstrations in mathematics.

A Practicing Catholic

We may wonder how Descartes, a practicing Catholic, could be so skeptical about traditional thinking when belief in the Church is a matter of accepting tradition. The answer is that he placed his faith in one airtight compartment and his reason in another. There was to be no interchange between the two. For St. Augustine, St. Thomas, and Newman there was always an interchange. Faith and reason were two wings on the same bird. Both were to beat in harmony. Descartes was a different kind of bird. He was shrewd enough, however, to mask his revolutionary intentions from the theologians of the University of Paris, the guardians of orthodoxy in the Church especially ready to repress the Protestant innovations introduced by Father Martin Luther in 1517. The Augustinian Monk had no use for Aristotle or St. Thomas Aquinas. Neither did Descartes. But the Frenchman maintained that his innovations in metaphysics would provide a better way to refute atheists because his demonstrations were based on a mathematical model, unlike those of St. Thomas Aquinas who, following Aristotle, used a physical model with its foundations in sense knowledge as the starting point of metaphysics.

Descartes claimed that his metaphysics would help the Church. Some influential ecclesiastics believed him, an influence that Pope Leo XIII later resisted by making St. Thomas Aquinas the Common Doctor of the Church in the late 1870's. The Pope was determined to eradicate the Cartesian strain that had entered Catholic philosophy and theology.

Seduce Us

Now let us observe how Descartes tries to seduce us from our common sense. He gives one of his reasons for not using the existence of bodies in the world as a starting point of philosophy. After dreaming that he is in his study, he wakes up to find himself in his bedroom. Now, he could have gotten up, dashed some cold water on his face, and become certain that he was in his bedroom. But he has already resolved to doubt everything that can be doubted. As a philosopher, he entertains the possibility that he might be still dreaming. Has he not had the experience of thinking he was awake when he was really dreaming? Could he be dreaming when he thinks he is awake? He has a doubt.

The doubt leaves two possibilities. If real bodies are the cause of the images in his mind, then waking up in his bedroom is because he is actually in his bedroom. His senses report truly. On the other hand, if the mind alone is the cause of the impression of being in his bedroom, he may still be dreaming. Do not drunks see pink elephants, drug users feel snakes crawling over them, or dreamers envision all kinds of things that are not real? Since he refuses to take the natural approach of saying that being awake in his bedroom is enough to tell him that he is in his bedroom, not his study, he must find another way to tell the difference. In his mind are the images of being in his study and of being in his bedroom. How will he decide which image gives him the truth of the situation?

The Judge

He will make the fatal move of using pure reason to serve as the judge. His use of reason will be pure because he has cut it off from its natural connection with sense knowledge. It is disembodied, detached. He will ask us to suspend our certitude that there is a bodily world and follow him down another path. He does not ask us to deny absolutely that there is a bodily world. He asks us only to refrain from assenting to it. In that way, he hopes we will give his argument a fair hearing. That is the way that I as a beginning philosopher interpreted him. I would be perfectly open-minded, a common mistake made by young philosophers like myself. But before we accompany him, let us consider the path we take when reasoning in a natural way.

If we had been momentarily confused about whether we were awake or asleep, we would have pinched ourselves, opened our eyes wider, dashed some cold water on our faces. After that, we would confidently conclude that we were in our bedroom, not in our study. Case closed. Another example: Let us suppose we are driving along a desert highway for the first time and see water ahead. We keep driving and find our impression to be only a mirage. More sense experience has made the correction. Or suppose that we are kids poking a stick into the water for the first time and see that it is bent. We pull it out and see that it is straight. We have begun to learn something about the refraction of light in water. Again, more sense experience has given us the truth of the situation. Despite appearances to the contrary, we learn without any doubt that we are awake, that the water on the road is a mirage, or that the stick is really straight. We don't have to resort to any high flying philosophy or metaphysics to get the facts.

Prompt Us

This experience may prompt us to wonder about the nature of sense knowledge. How is it that a body is aware of other bodies outside of it? It will take many a page of reading Aristotle or Aquinas to get the answer. While we may have great difficulty getting the right explanation (epistemology is not easy), we will hold onto the fact that we have knowledge about things in the world, just as Aristotle and Aquinas did. The difficulty in explaining the fact should not lead us to explain it away. Why should we give up our certitude about plain facts because of our inability to explain them philosophically? Now while there are people who are really confused about being asleep or awake, drunk or sober, we figure that they should not be readers of philosophy. They should see a doctor. We are not being contemptuous of them; we're just recognizing that they need help.

His Refusal

Descartes refuses to take the natural approach. Why? Because he is a philosopher with a high regard for mathematical demonstrations. For example, given that a triangle is a three-sided figure, we can demonstrate all the properties it must have. It is a plane or two-dimensional figure studied in plane geometry. In solid geometry, there are pyramids, cubes and cylinders, three-dimensional figures. Would it be possible to reduce natural bodies to just three dimensions? If one could, one would have a new approach to studying the bodily world. One would have a mathematician's approach. Can Descartes win our approval of it?

Beguiled

If we have been beguiled by Descartes, we have withheld our assent to the proposition that the bodily world exists. We have placed ourselves in a neutral zone. Instead of following our ordinary way of taking another look at an event which has puzzled us, thus resolving the puzzle by means of more sense experience, let's follow Descartes as he lowers us deeper into the pit of skepticism.

> I suppose. . .that whatever things I see are illusions; I believe that that none of the things my lying memory represents to have happened really did so; I have no sense; body, shape, extension, motion, place are chimeras. What then is true? Perhaps only this one thing, that nothing is certain. (p. 66)

He supposes for the sake of argument that he is not a body and has no knowledge of other bodies. He is facing utter and absolute skepticism, the death of all science and philosophy. It is also the death of all tradition, of the truth about everything that has happened in the past. In this blackout, it seems as if nothing is absolutely certain. Descartes has given real assent to the proposition that the senses are often deceptive. Feeling the pain of the uncertainty gives him the drive for a solution. In doing so he has left the path that human beings usually take and finds himself headed for a bottomless pit where nothing is certain. Consequently, he asks himself the following question:

> How do I know, however, that there is not something different from all the things I mentioned, as to which there is the least shadow of a doubt? (p. 66)

Having placed his natural certitude in suspension, he is in a very painful place. A bottomless pit of skepticism looms beneath his feet. Is there no way he can save himself? Is there anything that is certain, that is more than a possibility or a probability? That's the question. He proceeds to answer

An Interlude

it by taking all the final steps down to the bottom of the pit.

> Is there a God (or whatever I call him) who gives me these very thoughts? But why, on the other hand, should I think so? Perhaps I myself may be the author of them. --Well, am I, at any rate, one of them? --'But I have already said I have no senses and have no body—'At this point I stick; what follows from this? Am I so bound to a body and its senses that without them I cannot exist? --'But I have convinced myself that nothing in the world exists—no skies, no earth, no minds no bodies. So am I likewise non-existent?' But if I did convince myself of anything, I must have existed. 'But there is some deceiver, supremely powerful, supremely intelligent, who purposely always deceives me. 'If he deceives me, then again I undoubtedly exist; let him deceive me as much as he may, he will never bring it about that, at the time of thinking that I am something, I am in fact nothing. *Thus I have already weighed all considerations enough and more than enough; and must conclude that this proposition 'I am', 'I exist', whenever I utter or conceive it in my mind, is necessarily true.* [my italics] (p. 67)

He claims to have rescued himself from utter skepticism by the use of his disembodied reason. He says: "I think, therefore, I am" (Cogito ergo sum). Whether he is right or wrong, sober or drunk, clean or drugged, he knows he exists. Even a deceiving God could not talk him out of that truth. He attained it by looking at himself. He did not learn it by seeing a tree, by hearing the birds singing in it, or by smelling the blossoms and concluding that he exists because he could sense the tree. No! The proof that he exists is that he can think. He is an unextended, spiritual thing or substance not attached to a body or to a world of bodies. Having attained a clear idea of who he is, he is now in a position to deduce the properties that must flow from his essence or nature. Just as a geometrician is able to deduce the properties of cubes and cylinders from a clear idea of their essence, he will do so from the clear idea of his own essence.

Pause for a Moment

Let us pause for a moment to reflect upon what Descartes has done. He thinks he has saved himself from utter skepticism by connecting his thought with something that is undoubtedly real—himself. We as realists can agree. We do not have to demonstrate to ourselves that we exist. We know it immediately. The real question, however, is how we know it. Reflecting on our ordinary experience of the world, we see that it is bodies themselves that we see, smell, hear, or touch while as the same time being aware that it is we who are doing the seeing, smelling, hearing, or touching. In a thought experiment, however, let us imagine that we were in a deep coma. While there would still be a tree of sweet-smelling blossoms with birds singing in it, we would not be conscious of it. While there would still be waves of color, odor and sound washing over us, we would be inert, unresponsive. The point? We need our senses working to be aware. This is what our analysis of ordinary experience reveals. Remove the activity of our senses and we remove any awareness of ourselves. There is no Self or essence from which we can deduce its properties. Of course, in our minds we can do a head trip of divesting ourselves of colors, sounds, and smells in order to arrive at a pure unextended self that exists as a kind of angel. But that's a head trip. It's a kind of fantasy we can concoct, not an insight into the way our knowing things really goes.

Holds On

Yet Descartes holds on to his theory. From the fact that he exists he makes some amazing deductions. First, since he is an unextended substance, he has no parts. Thus he cannot fall apart. Therefore, he must be immortal. Second, since he has the idea of an Infinite God in his mind, he cannot be the cause of it because he is only a finite agent. Therefore, God must be the cause of it. Thus, God exists. Third, since God must be good, He cannot be a deceiver. Hence he can trust the sense powers God has given him. He has come by the method of demonstration to the long deferred conclusion that the three dimensional world exists. Yet this is not the world he left when he began. While the world he left had three dimensions, it had a lot more. There were bodies that were essentially different from each other. There were plants that existed as rocks did but had the characteristic of being living bodies. And there were animals that were living but also have the characteristic of having senses. Finally, there was man who had senses but also the characteristic of having reason. By his method of doubting sense knowledge, however, he has reduced the bodily world to one only of cubes or cylinders.

Why?

Why was Descartes so intent on reducing the world of bodies to three dimensions? It was because it allowed him to take a mathematical approach to the natural world. Man the agent, the Great Engineer, can then create blue prints in his mind and then impose them on the formless matter of three dimensions. Formerly plants served as the food for animals. Now man himself can design the food and produce super animals. There is no limit to how far he can go. And why should he not be able to make super athletes who will be able to do what no athlete has done before? The possibilities are endless for the Great Engineer.

A Few More Examples

Formerly, a man was a man, a woman was a woman, and a baby a baby. Let us suppose today that a man born a male wants to be a female. He can go to a surgeon, who cuts off some parts and adds others. The transformation is not perfect but it is close enough. Suppose a person born a female wants to be a male. A surgeon can make the change. The result may not be perfect but it will become better in the future. There are no limits to the possibilities of science. Again: A baby is conceived at an inconvenient time. It can be cut out like a cancer cell. But suppose the couple wants the baby. Then it remains a baby. It all depends how you wish to fill an empty three dimensional cylinder. Seeing it has a cancer cell makes it a cancer cell. Seeing it as baby makes it a baby. Such freedom was unimaginable in the days when mathematics was not yet integrated with the sciences. In the modern age, there will be many more possibilities. Suppose a man wishes to live to three or four hundred years old. Although science cannot make that promise today, it can freeze his body so that when science improves, the corpse can be unfrozen and given the right ingredients. Why not?

Descartes was working on creating a science which would vastly increase his life span. Being afraid, however, that he would die before he completed his science, he wrote a shorter version of it. As things turned out, he died at the age of fifty-four due to a respiratory infection caused by teaching Queen Christiana at her preferred time of five o'clock in the morning.

An Interlude

The Spirit of Descartes

The spirit of Descartes lives on today. Essential to that spirit is the reliance on pure reason as exemplified when mathematics is applied to the various sciences of politics, sociology, biology, chemistry, physics, and the rest. The more a body of knowledge lends itself to be counted and measured, the more scientific it is supposed to be. The study of statistics becomes a necessity. The ordinary knowledge acquired by considering the colors, sounds, tastes, and textures of things is thrown out the window. The teachings of faith are especially to be condemned. Truth is encased in abstract mathematical formulas.

Having Seen

Having seen the importance Descartes gives to his view that he is a Self which thinks, a kind of angel or pure spirit, let us retrace our steps by taking the stance of a philosophical realist. Does a consideration of the information attained by sense knowledge warrant the conclusion that we are Unextended Selves or spirits? To answer that question, let us examine the facts of ordinary experience. Let us go back to the tree in our yard again. Let us imagine a tree in our yard filled with sweet smelling pink blossoms and singing birds. While our focus is centered on the tree, we are aware that we are sensing it. But it is the actual tree that we focus on. We can, however, step back and reflect that we see pink blossoms with our eyes, hear singing birds with our ears, smell the perfumed blossoms with our noses and feel the tree trunk with our hands. That's our experience analyzed into its parts. We now have in us the image of a body with colors, sounds, odors, and denseness and also a reflective awareness of how we have come by this image. The more time we spend in observing the tree, the better is our image of the tree and of ourselves observing it. Now suppose we were blind, deaf, clogged up, and perfectly numb. What would we sense? Nothing! Would we be still aware that we existed? No. We can detect no pure self, existing independently of the sensations we have coming in from the outside or from inside our bodies. Without sensations coming in, we would be unaware, unconscious, complete zero's. We would not know we had a body because we would not be aware of any Self to have one. We only become aware of ourselves in the act of sensing bodies. We don't have to reason to that plain fact. We don't have to infer it. For with every normal experience of sensation we are aware both of things in the world and of ourselves sensing them. This is what an analysis of ordinary experience shows.

Like and Unlike Aristotle

Like Aristotle, Newman holds that there is an identity between the knower and the known. But Newman does not go into any proof of it. Aristotle does. He starts out with respect for ordinary experience. First he points out that bodies affect each other physically by means of heat and light waves reflecting off each other. Non-sentient bodies of course are not aware of being affected. Animals are. A cow is aware of the green and sweet-smelling grass around it. In doing so, it does not get any fatter and the grass remains. The case would be different if the cow ate the grass. The cow would undergo a physical change and the grass would be destroyed. But when the cow merely senses the grass, we may say that it becomes the grass, not physically, but cognitionally. It is only aware of it.

Let's take an example closer to home. We see a juicy steak on our plate and smell its aroma. We do not get fatter and the steak remains as it was. We are only aware of it. We identify

An Interlude

with it cognitionally. There are two stages here. The first is the fact that bodies affect each other physically. No knowledge or awareness on their part is involved. A rock is not aware of the heat waves affecting it due to the effects upon it generated by other rocks. The second stage is that bodies with senses (animals) become aware of other bodies when they sense them. Although an animal's sensing of bodies starts with purely physical factors, it leads to awareness or consciousness. Our sense organs have that kind of power.

Our Experience

Our experience today confirms Aristotle's explanation. We do not say that the electronic machines used to detect light or sound actually see or hear anything. The sensors that department stores put on their doors so that they open when a customer approaches do not see anything. The sensors that the army uses to detect the sounds of tanks moving beneath the canopy of a jungle do not hear anything. They are merely tools registering physical changes. It is the men using these tools that do the seeing and the hearing. Man's possession of sense powers enables him to be aware of bodies by means of the color waves affecting his eyes and the sound waves affecting his ears. In this regard, he is an animal. But he is also a rational animal. Thus, he is able to create devices to supplement the organs of his eyes and ears. Brute animals are incapable of this feat.

Note

Note the kind of evidence we have used in our explanation. It is no better and no worse than that used by the ancient Greeks. We have drawn it from the difference between the way cows react to grass and the way rocks are affected by other rocks. While the tools of modern science give us a much better idea of the physical factors involved in being aware or conscious, they do not tell us what exactly consciousness is. All that we know is what Aristotle knew; namely that we are conscious of the existence of bodies by means of our sense powers. We can make robots. But we can't make cockroaches or cats with their ability to move about. Cats and cockroaches live; computers and robots don't. The day when scientists can manufacture living things in their labs using only non-living material will be the day we can dismiss the ancient Greeks. Until then, we must heed their explanations of why sentient bodies behave as they do. We must be content with common sense observations of the way bodies appear to us.

Consider the Following

Consider the modern situation. Many today consider a human being to be a Self, divided into males with one set of plumbing, females with another set, and neuters with no plumbing at all. But with the help of surgeons, males can be changed into females, females can be changed into males, or those disgusted with sex into neuters. The changes is not yet perfect but will get better as science progresses. But those with a more powerful sense of Self can skip the surgeons, form a voting bloc, and demand that the government pass laws which allow them to behave in any manner they think appropriate as far as rest rooms, locker rooms, and bedrooms are concerned. Descartes of course would be horrified at such an outcome. But it was he who set the Western World on the path that modern elites have taken. Casting doubt on the certitude which ordinary folk have on the existence of bodies differentiated into mineral, vegetative, sentient, or rational, they made them just three dimensional. Why then should not a Self have the power to take any material form it desires? If Descartes can take the notion of a Self and deduce the properties of being immortal, God-believing, and sense-trusting, why cannot a modern be anything that he, she, or it wants to be? Descartes "liberated" human reason from being bound by the facts supplied by sense knowledge and made it a kind of god. Why should a god be bound to what it does not wish to be bound? Why should it be bound by limitations it has not freely chosen? Should not free choice rule nature?

Newman's Method

We are now in a position to compare Newman's method with those of philosophical idealists like Descartes. Unlike Descartes, he takes for granted that man lives in a world of bodies. Having experience of them, he has a definite storehouse of facts he can use to reason about. One conclusion is that we give our unconditional assent to propositions like Great Britain's being an island or Moscow's being a city in Russia even though we have never been in either of those places. Although our inferences about the trustworthiness of those who claim to be eyewitnesses are only probable, we give our assent unconditionally. Without needing any further explanation we know we have the truth about these concrete matters.

Again, Newman holds as a certainty that the apprehension of things moves our imagination more than our apprehension of notions does. Such is the plain fact. While he could have gone on to explain it more fully, he does not need that kind of full explanation to establish the fact. On the contrary, the only fact the philosophical idealist will admit to is the existence of notions in his mind, not the existence of things in the world. His doubts have placed a gap between him and the world. Considering himself as a mind without a body, he needs a philosophical argument to get back his body again. Having discarded the senses, he relies on the mind alone to bring him back to reality. But it is a reality of which he will be the creator. Using mathematical physics as a tool, he can dream of making a heaven or earth. Is he not a god? This approach is a long way from the example of a mother and child showing that our most fundamental act is to trust in the word of our mothers. It is real assent to the trustworthiness of a beloved authority that explains how all human beings operate. Before we exercise our powers of inferring, we are already believers.

No Difference

As far as the relationship of Newman to philosophical realists like Aristotle are concerned, there is no difference in the starting points. They take for granted that man has sense knowledge of individual bodies in the worlds. Upon this starting point, Aristotle builds a philosophy or metaphysics explaining why the facts are so by locating their ultimate causes. He gives a definitive treatment to the matter. His explanations are timeless, meaning they hold for all persons in all times and in all places. In contrast, Newman is writing *An Essay in Aid of a Grammar of Assent.* It is an essay, an attempt to investigate the topic of assent in a culture trying to forget its past. The modern age has succeeded in confusing people, especially the educated, about the difference between knowing a fact and explaining it. Due to the influence of philosophers like Descartes, the fact that there is a bodily world serving as the basic standard by which we can tell the difference between a good definition or a poor one is thrown into doubt.

In the midst of this confusion in an apocalyptic age, Newman addresses Catholics first because they will hold out as a society, a flock, that will have divine aid in resisting the disintegration of religion, philosophy, and common sense. Does not a Catholic hold that before the bread and wine becomes the Body and Blood of Christ, the host is really bread and the wine really wine? There is no Cartesian doubt here. Furthermore, Newman addresses Catholics who have gone to college. While this minority takes its place in the pews alongside the majority of their unlearned brethren, it also has the duty of getting back to the proper philosophical roots, the facts of ordinary experience. Accordingly, Newman pounds away at presenting the facts, taking great care not to distract himself and others with metaphysical explanations which, although true, will lose or confuse typical graduates of secularized institutions. In presenting fact after fact after fact, he will also present the grammar, the vocabulary, to express the facts so that graduates can communicate with each other and form schools of thought that are sane.

Newman is blazing a new trail in a culture that has suffered a disaster. There are no basic facts or ordinary experience to appeal to, unlike the situation in ancient and medieval times when people took for granted that a baby is a baby, a man a man and a woman a woman. They had a solid platform from which the philosophers like Aquinas could launch investigations into what was beyond the physical. Newman deems it would be a waste of effort to do that in the modern age. So, as we have seen in the sermon, he addresses himself as a Catholic to other Catholics. Faith is our rock of certainty. But it is not the type of faith that flies on one wing alone. This faith also has the wing of reason. The proper use of reason plants everybody in a world of bodies whether they want to be there or not. Modern man does not want such clarity. This attitude affects our imagination, especially those of us who have the opportunity for higher education. We have to get a hold of ourselves as human beings. To do that we need a grammar, a vocabulary, to support and express to each other our identity as human beings in a culture that does not want to be human. It wants to be above the human condition. One of the illusions we have to dispel is that the assent of belief is restricted just to religious matters. To hold this position is tantamount to denying the basic fact that human beings start their lives as believers in the word of their parents. Thus in order to see religious matters in their proper light, he first has to show ordinary matters in their proper light.

Step of the Argument

The comparison between Newman and Descartes shows the contrast between a philosophical realist and a philosophical idealist. The realist gives priority to the existence of individual persons and things in the world. What exists in the world is the standard used to evaluate the images and notions we have of it. The process takes time. Here the mind must conform to the way the world is. In contrast, idealists gives priority to the images and notions of things and persons as they exist in the mind. Man, the Great Engineer, becomes the standard of truth. The difficulty is that while men in an apocalyptic age have united in repressing realists, they will oppose each other ferociously. Who among the gods will be the chief god? Whose blueprints will prevail? The result of this struggle will be a hell on earth, a war among the gods.

Chapter Six

Apprehension of Propositions (Chapter Three of the *Essay*)

We have ranged far and wide in investigating the philosophical differences between idealists and realists. Let us now get back to work and follow Newman going step by step and sticking to the facts. He develops the distinction he has already made between real and notional apprehension of propositions. Like an English bulldog, he sinks his teeth into the facts of real apprehension and holds on. He starts again with an analysis of language, a tedious but necessary step.

> I have used the word *apprehension*, and not *understanding*, because the latter word is of uncertain meaning, sometimes for the faculty or act of conceiving a proposition, sometimes for the act of comprehending, neither of which comes into the sense of *apprehension. It is possible to apprehend without understanding.* [my italics] I apprehend what is meant by saying that John is Richard's wife's father's aunt's husband, but, if I am unable to understand the upshot of the whole, viz. that John is great-uncle-in-law to Richard, I cannot be said to understand the proposition. (p. 20)

We can use the term "understanding" to refer to the faculty by which we understand things. Or we can refer to the act by which this faculty understands. None of these usages suits Newman. To illustrate, he gives the example that John is such and such. We apprehend the meaning of the words without comprehending the meaning of the whole sentence. He goes on further to explain, saying:

> In like manner, I may take a just view of a man's conduct, and therefore apprehend it, and yet profess that I do not understand it; that is, I have not have the key to it, and do not see its consistency in detail. *Apprehension then is simply an intelligent acceptance of the idea, or of the fact which a proposition enunciates.* [my italics] "Pride will have a fall"; "Napoleon died at St. Helena"; I have no difficulty in entering into the sentiment of the former of these, or into the fact declared in the later; that is, I apprehend them both. (p. 20)

We have apprehension of the fact that a judge with a reputation for honesty took a bribe. But we don't comprehend the situation until we understand its cause. Perhaps he was adept at practicing the appearance of honesty rather than its realty and finally got caught. Knowing that, we would have the key to comprehending the behavior of the judge.

Similarly, we can apprehend the notion of pride having a fall without comprehending it. If, however, we take a fall because of our pride, we will then have the experience that illuminates the notion. We will comprehend it. Again, we can apprehend the fact that Napoleon died on St. Helena without comprehending the significance of this event in history. But when we learn the significance of Napoleon's death in the context of European history, we have the fact explained in terms of its cause. We then have comprehension.

A Distinction

Newman has taken great pains to distinguish between apprehending a thing or a notion and comprehending it. Why? Because ordinary experience tells us that we know many facts without understanding their causes. For example, we know for a fact that Great Britain is an island without comprehending all the causes of the fact. Again, we have many notions in our mind like "pride," "honesty," or "cause" without realizing how they relate to each other. Initially, our apprehension of notions is half-baked. We attain comprehension only when we see how the notions explain the facts. To stress the point, we know many historical facts like Napoleon's dying on the island of St. Helena. But if we do not make the effort to understand the significance of this event in the history of Europe, we lack comprehension.

Why this great effort of Newman to point out the obvious? The reason is that he is aware that idealists like Descartes start philosophizing by refusing to give their assent to the fact that we are bodies with a basic knowledge of other bodies. With such a starting point the apprehension of plain facts disappears. Newman counters Descartes' first principle with the observation that we know for a fact that there are not only bodies in the world but that we are bodies as well. This knowledge in itself, however, does not include knowledge of the causes of the fact. It only provides a foundation upon which we can build knowledge of the causes, knowledge that results in comprehension. Thus, we have the distinction between apprehension of the facts and comprehension of their causes. Just because we do not have comprehension of the causes working in the world is no reason to deny the fact that there is a bodily world. It is this basic apprehension of bodies that leads us on to seek the comprehension of its causes.

An Objective Standard

The real apprehension of things gives us an objective standard to hold onto when seeking the causes of things. Whatever the explanation, we know for a fact that the judge took a bribe, that pride precedes a fall, or that Napoleon died on St. Helena's. But if we do not assume sense knowledge of these facts, we have no anchor to hold us steady as we search for the causes. The idealist has no such anchor. As a substitute, Descartes uses the vividness or clarity of the image or idea impressing the imagination or the intellect.

But people due to their character vary in what impresses them. Mathematicians cherish the clarity of pure geometrical figures like globes or cubes over the density of diamonds, trees, horses, or men. Drunks have far more awareness of pink elephants rather than of real elephants. Making the vividness of an image or the clarity of a notion opens up the door to all kinds of subjective views. The apprehension of ordinary facts gets lost, thus leaving idealists in a private world instead of being in the same world with everybody else.

More Examples

Newman gives more examples of the way we distinguish between notional and real apprehension. In the case of grammarians and orators, the apprehension is notional because they are concerned with the relations of terms to each other like words to propositions, predicates to subjects, or premises to conclusions. Speakers are in control of arranging these forms. The reader can sit back, passively expecting clarity in the exposition. It is the job of the logician or the orator to be clear in the management of ideas. But in the case of an experimentalist, readers must make an effort to enter into his mind because he is using words and propositions to describe things. Listeners cannot just rely only on the words or the propositions. They must bestir themselves to understand the things behind the words. Since the readers and the experimentalist are living in the same physical world, they have something in common. Readers can then examine that world for themselves and then compare the result with the account of the experimentalist. They must be more active, more willing to forgive a certain inaccuracy or variation in the use of terms because matching the right words to the tremendous complexity found in the real world is no easy task.

Newman's Argument

Newman's whole argument supplies a good example of the difference between an orator and an experimentalist. While

Newman uses his skill as a literary man to put his argument into a logical and persuasive order, he is intent on using words to indicate what goes on in the real world. To catch his meaning, we have to focus on our own experience of the world. In doing so, however, we already have our own frames of interpretation. For instance, mine is that of an Aristotelian and Thomist trained in Scholasticism. I have been accustomed to a particular way of using words to express my insight into reality. While Newman is well-informed about Aristotle and Aquinas, he has his own way of using words which is more characteristic of a literary education than one in the formal way of Scholasticism. In the final analysis, I have been forced to consult my own experience of what is meant by sensation, intellection, or syllogizing due to Newman's use of examples. Some of them don't touch me at all. I am not an Englishman of the Nineteenth Century. Others hit deeper. And so I find myself inquiring once again into exactly what goes on when I give my assent to the truth of a proposition. Reading Newman has forced me to take another look at the world which prompted Aristotle and Aquinas to explain it their way. In the final analysis, seeking the truth about the way of the world is as personal to us as are our own fingerprints. No one else has the same set. Yet each set does indeed give us the knowledge that we are in the same world.

A Schoolboy

He draws an example contrasting a schoolboy and an economist. A clever boy can do a credible job of translating a treatise in economics from one language to another and yet know very little about economics. In a similar vein, Newman recalls his own experience of examinations testing his knowledge of grammar by translating passages from the classics. The point of the examination was not to grasp the full meaning of the passage. It was to test the ability of the student to distinguish between the use of the ablative and dative case, a study in the relations of words to each other. But the point of an author's words is to get his readers into the shoes of some great hero. Once the reader gets into the reality of the hero, the words of the author have done what they were supposed to do.

Again: Perhaps you know something about medicine. There are the Latin and Greek derivatives describing diseases or procedures. We can apprehend these notions without comprehending the whole scheme of the sciences of medicine or surgery. Further, we can apprehend the science in such a detached way as to forget how painful and bloody diseases and surgeries are. We have to join our apprehension of the notions to our apprehension of the facts in order to comprehend the whole situation.

Summary

Newman summarizes as follows:

> Such are the two modes of apprehension. The terms of a proposition do or do not stand for things. If they do they are singular terms, for all things that are, are units. But if they do not stand for things they must stand for notions, and are common nouns. Singular nouns come from experience, common from abstraction. The apprehension of the former I call real, and of the later notional. (p. 22)

Other Modes of Real Apprehension

The bodily world is real and therefore quite rich. While it has the power to impress us in the present, it also has the power to affect us when it is not present. May not a melody heard in the past or a scent recalled still have the power to move us? This topic brings up the power of memory. Memories of seeing things seem to be more vivid than memories of sounds. Yet old songs also have evocative power. But there is a limit. If we haven't heard a melody, no verbal description will enable us to hear it. Again, if we have never smelled roses, no description will be able us to have the experience.

But what about things like huge fires, tremendous earth quakes, or great battles we have not experienced? If we have a good imagination, we can still have a real apprehension of them. Indeed, some authors have such great powers of composition that they can give a more impressive account of a battle they were never in than those who have actually been in the battle.

Implicit in Newman's account is that real apprehensions are *personal* while notional apprehensions are *impersonal*. The reason is that everybody has his own body with his own set of eyes and ears and his own existence in time and place. Thus, his perceptions are never exactly the same as anybody else's because his images are not exactly the same. It makes a big difference whether the perceiver has been blind from birth or been blinded later on. Again some people are color blind or shortsighted. Others are hard of hearing. On the contrary, notional apprehensions are impersonal. No matter who speaks of rocks, plants, or animals in general, a rock is inorganic, a plant organic, or an animal an organic body with senses. Here we have the sameness that makes communication possible.

More Explicit

Newman makes more explicit what he has assumed from the beginning; namely that each of us is the source of the questions we ask, the inferences we draw, and the assents we give. The real assent we give as children to the words and example of our parents provides the lens through which we see the world. Our character is influenced, an influence which shapes our intellectual activities. Religious parents will shape one type of character, non-religious parents another. Newman illustrates:

> Thus we meet with men of the world who cannot enter into the very idea of devotion, and think, for instance, that, from the nature of the case, a life of religious seclusion must be either one of unutterable dreariness or abandoned sensuality, because they know of no exercise of the affections but what is merely human; and with others again, who, living in the home of their own

selfishness, ridicule as something fanatical and pitiable the self-sacrifices of generous high-mindedness and chivalrous honour. They cannot create images of these things, any more than children on the contrary can of vice, when they ask whereabouts and who the bad men are; for they have no personal memories, and have to content themselves with notions drawn from books or from what others tell them. *So much on the apprehension of things and on the real in our use of language . . .* (p. 27)

In comparing the real assent of a worldly person to that of a religious person, Newman dramatizes the fact that people can live in the same physical world and yet live in different worlds as far as religious and moral matters go. Children brought up by parents who are hostile or indifferent to religion will have one way of viewing the world. Children brought up by religious parents will have another way. There will be an instinctive opposition between them when they meet in society. Since the culture of the modern age will be hostile or indifferent to religion, there will be unavoidable conflict. The difference will be shown in arguments about the nature of the state, the law, or the constitution, but they will only be symptoms of the difference, not the real causes. The real causes are what people love or hate, seek or avoid. These are beyond the reach of argument. They set the presuppositions from which arguments start.

Subject Matter of Notional Apprehension

Newman proceeds to a few basic points about notional apprehension, the realm in which scientists and philosophers dwell. As we go about sensing the particular things existing in the world, we spontaneously reduce them to various kinds of things in our minds so that we are able to compare and contrast them with each other. Even a student in high school can do this. He can see that men are similar to dogs in being animals but are different in being rational. Again, he can see that dogs are similar to trees in being living bodies but different in having senses. He can see that trees

Apprehension of Propositions

are similar to rocks in being bodies but different in being living bodies. Thus the process of placing individual things in various categories like rational bodies, sentient bodies, living bodies and plain bodies is easy for a student if his teachers bothers to instruct him in the basics of grammar and logic. It was this spontaneous and informal systemization of ideas that Aristotle used as his basis for logic. As Newman puts it: "We apprehend spontaneously, even before we set about apprehending that man is like man, yet unlike; and unlike a horse, a tree, a mountain or a monument." (p. 27) Man can then turn his gaze away from individual things and consider only his ideas or notions which, of course, exist only in his mind. Newman's comment on the process is as follows:

> In processes of this kind we regard things, *not as they are in themselves, but mainly as they stand in relation to each other.* [my italics] We look at nothing simply for its own sake; we cannot look at one thing without keeping our eyes on a multitude of other things besides. 'Man' is no longer what he really is, an individual presented to us by our senses, but as we read him in the light of those comparisons and contrasts which we have made him suggest to us. He is attenuated into an aspect, or relegated to his place in a classification. Thus his appellation is made to suggest, not the real being which he is in this or that specimen of himself, but a definition. If I might use a harsh metaphor, I should say he is made the logarithm of his true self, and in that shape is worked with the ease and satisfaction of logarithms. (p. 27)

The comparison between defining something and reducing it to a logarithm of its true self is harsh. Newman admits it. Is he then calling his definitions of questioning, inferring, and assenting mere logarithms or starved down notions of these activities in the real world? Of course not! But that is because he has already done the spadework of considering these activities as they take place in the real world. He has examined the facts from which he has drawn his definitions. He can then claim that he has zeroed in on the essential characteristics of these activities. His readers have not necessarily done so. Instead, they may have just bare notions, mere logarithms in their minds. They must then apply these to their own experience to get a better grip on them.

Implicit

Implicit in Newman's contrasting notional and real apprehension is his sense of the power of the concrete order. Through sense knowledge, we are clued into actual bodies that change in place and time. We sense them as they are at one moment and see what happens to them at the next. Thus, we are in for many surprises because events do not turn out as expected. Chance intervenes. Hidden causes become apparent. Reality busts through appearances. While our sense of them at any given moment is certain, we cannot take our eye off of them as if they will be that way when we look at them again. In order to keep our balance in the midst of a changing world, we zero in on the essential characteristics of bodies, define their natures, and learn the properties that necessarily follow. We take a philosophical or scientific view of them to detect the order underlying the constant flow of development or dissolution, as the case may be. But if we wish to know what happens to a particular thing minute by minute, we have to keep our eyes and ears on it minute by minute.

If we were angels we would not have to put up with this suspense. As theologians tell us, we would see things as a whole. But we are not angels. We are spirits operating in a body. We have to learn about things day by day, year by year. There are those surprises, either happy or sad. It is with our senses that we keep up with the ebb and flow of the world. By the use of reason, we can keep focused on the overriding purpose of the world and of our own purpose in it. This steadiness of vision, which is notional, helps us keep our balance. Otherwise, we might fall into the depressing thought that history is just one damned thing after another.

Newman's Comment

Newman has said that notions may be just the logarithm of things, a pale imitation of real things. True enough. But they still have their place. He says:

> Each use of propositions [notional and real] has its own usefulness and serviceableness, and each has its own imperfection. To apprehend notionally is to have breadth of mind, but to be shallow. To apprehend really is to be deep, but to be narrow-minded. The latter is the conservative principle of knowledge, and the former the principle of its advancement. Without the apprehension of notions, we should forever pace round one small circle of knowledge; without a firm hold upon things, we should waste ourselves in vague speculations. However, *real apprehension has the precedence, as being the scope and end and test* [my italics] of the notional; and the fuller is the mind's hold upon things or what it considers such, the more fuller is it in its aspects of them, and the more practical in its definitions. (p. 29-30)

Individual things existing in the world and their activities are the basic realities. Sense knowledge puts us in direct contact with them. Even an animal senses the differences among a rock, a plant, another animal, or a man. But it has no grasp of their general nature, of their various kinds. Only man, a rational animal, is able to know their various kinds or natures and then put them into words like definitions. But while it is an achievement to be able to define things, the definitions only give us their essential natures. In the real world, however, these natures have all kinds of accidental relations to other natures. There is the story of how King Richard the Second lost his life and his kingdom because the nails holding the shoes to the hooves of his horse failed. Who would have ever thought that the work of a blacksmith was so important? The man might have had a bad day because he had quarreled with his wife. Life holds many surprises for us, surprises that philosophy and science are unable to predict.

Yet there still is a place for liberal education where the young are taught to generalize and define in the sciences and arts. They become broader in their views. They go beyond the confines of their personal experience in learning how to think in the big world. But unless they fill in those scientific, philosophical, theological, or literary generalizations with the experience of life, they risk being mere theorists, great windbags full of talk and notions with hardly an ounce of common sense in them.

Real apprehension is the conservative principle of knowledge. It gives men roots. It makes them deep—but not necessarily right. Whatever they choose as their goal in life—whether it be pleasure, wealth, honor, or virtue—they do so with passion. In contrast, a liberal education is the principle of advancement in knowledge. It puts people beyond their personal experience out into the big world where they can communicate with each other in a way that animals can't. Of course, the barking of wolves tells their fellows something about where the prey is. But do we wish to equate the exchanges between professors and students with the barking of a hunting pack?

Expressed here is Newman's view of a liberal education. He takes for granted that young adults do not have enough experience of life to digest the information they have gathered in courses like the history of Western Civilization. Such exposure broadens their horizons, as one might expect from a university education. They learn that there is something about being human that is not confined to their own age. They acquire range.

But the quest for a philosophical habit of mind has its dangers. It is not possible for the student to maintain the connection between his experience of life and all the notions that pour in upon him. He is like a sloop trying to take on the sails of a man-of-war. While he must try to take on new rigging, he also has to take care to start building a larger ship of himself so that he can put enough ballast in the hold to carry all that sail. As a young man I used to feel that I could think myself around the disasters that come from the reckless pursuit of wine, women, and song. You just read a few classic books on how man should live and you think you have the virtues. It doesn't work that way. There is no short cut to acquiring virtue. You have to live it day after day for a long time. The knowledge of virtue does not come from reading arguments about it. It means holding out against the allurements of the world, the flesh and the devil. Here we are talking about truth as the object of real, not just of notional assent.

Return To the Argument

To return to the argument: In his discussion of the notional and real apprehension of propositions, Newman has provided us with the foundations underlying all further acts of assent. Before he can address questions about the relationship of assent to life in the big world, he first has to deal with life as man first encounters it in the rocks, trees, rabbits, and men he sees around him, thus giving him images of what is real, images which fill his imagination and memory. He then encounters it in the notions or ideas he derives from these things, thus supplying himself with ideas that he may then consider on their own terms. These ideas or notions by themselves do not move the imagination so much as they inform his mind. Yet, they also have a very important role to play. They are the basis of the sciences.

All in all, direct experience of things gives men their "insides" so to speak. Thus when they begin to ask questions about matters beyond their immediate experience, they have to rely upon the word of the more experienced and upon their own sense of what is probable. In brief, any realist's account of belief and inference starts from the fact that man already has knowledge, not just belief, of many things in the world. But it is basic beliefs that give him the ability to put together not only the commonwealth of the sciences but the elements of a good life.

Formal education is important. But the education provided

by the experience of life is even more important. The first type is notional. The second type is real. Students should appreciate the difference. But they can't. They have to enter the school of hard knocks before they start to get real.

Step of the Argument

By the use of many examples, Newman deepens our insight into the fact that notional apprehension deals with notions of things and real apprehension with things themselves. Notional apprehension supplies us with general ideas that enable us to communicate with each other about the kinds of things in the world. This apprehension is broad but not deep. Real apprehension supplies us with images giving each of us our personal reaction to individual bodies in the world. This apprehension is deep but quite narrow. It can also be quite wrong.

Chapter Seven

Notional and Real Assent (Chapter Four of the *Essay*)

As we have seen, an assent is either notional or real, notional when given to what is taken to be the truth of a notion, real when given to what is taken to be the truth of a thing. Real assent is stronger because it gets its power to move us from images in the imagination derived from things. Things or bodies are individual, unique. They impact us directly with images. Yet notional assent also has its place; it enables us to know the various *kinds* of things in the world through our ability to form concepts, abstractions, or definitions of bodies. We say, then, that man is a rational animal, an animal because he is in direct contact with bodies, and a rational one because of his ability to reason about *the kinds* of bodies. Put the two capabilities together and we have the single substance or body we understand to be a man.

Newman proceeds to mark off various types of notional assent. Since all of them are assents, they are unconditional or categorical propositions. But they have been preceded by five different types of inference that are of course conditional. For the fact is that we do not go around giving an assent without having to some extent reasoned to it. The types of reasoning or inferring are professing, believing, opining, presuming, and speculating. The assents are profession, credence, opinion, presumption, and speculation.

1) Profession (p. 34)

The first type of notional assent is profession. It is the most superficial. Nevertheless, it is still an unconditional hold on what is taken to be the truth of a notion. The hold in this case is quite feeble because the reasoning preceding it is superficial. It changes easily.

> There are assents so feeble and superficial, as to be little more than assertions. I class them all together under the heading of profession. Such are the assents made upon habit and without reflection; as when a man calls himself a Tory or a Liberal, as having been brought up as such...." (p. 34)

Because the predicates "Tory" or "Liberal" are general terms, they are notions. Because the propositions stated are unconditional, they are assents. The reasoning or inferring that precedes profession is a matter of unreflecting habit. A man says "I am a Tory," or "I am a Liberal," because that's what his father was. Again, a person may adopt a certain style of dress or a certain taste in novels because he or she is following popular fashions. The areas of politics and religion are also fertile fields where professions grow in abundance. Newman continues:

> *To say "I do not understand a proposition, but I accept it on authority," is not formalism, [profession] but faith; it is not a direct assent to the proposition, still it is an assent to the authority which enunciates it;* [my italics] but what I here speak of is professing to understand without understanding. It is thus that political and religious watchwords are created; first one man of name and then another adopts them, till their use becomes popular, and then every one professes them, because every one else does. Such words are "liberality," "progress," "light," "civilization;" such are "justification by faith only," "vital religion," "private judgment," "the Bible and nothing but the Bible." Such again are "Rationalism," "Gallicanism," "Jesuitism," "Ultramon-

tanism"—all of which, in the mouths of conscientious thinkers, have a definite meaning, but are used by the multitude as war-cries, nicknames, and shibboleths, with scarcely enough of the scantiest grammatical apprehension of them to allow of their being considered in truth more than assertions. (p. 35)

Newman speaks disapprovingly of those professing but not because they are believers. It is the human condition to believe a great many truths and untruths like sponges soaking in whatever is around them. We are social animals dependent upon each other for our survival and well-being. If in the course of our lives we didn't pay heed to what others say, we would not survive very long. A tribe living in lion country learns to defend its cattle with spears. We can imagine that the first spear throwers often got themselves killed. But after more experience, the spear throwers got more skillful and the lions got killed. Beginners imitating elders is a sound practice.

Here Newman is much more accepting of the human condition than Descartes. In beginning to philosophize, the Frenchman throws into doubt everything he has learned because it has come to him through senses which can make mistakes. Realists are not so fussy. In the quest for survival, they allow for a certain amount of trial and error. They are just fallible human beings, not gods. But Descartes doesn't want to be a mere human being. By his use of reason he resolves to doubt everything he has learned until all he has left is his reason alone, nothing more. He makes his reason the replacement for taking into account the tried and true experience of his elders. Like a teenager who considers himself to be the most unique person who has ever lived, he has to discover everything himself. He will be reinventing the wheel every chance he gets. If he keeps up that attitude, his chances for surviving as a normal human being are very slim.

2) Credence (p. 41)

Newman proceeds to describe the second form of notional

assent. "What I mean by giving credence to propositions is pretty much the same as having 'no doubt' about them.' " (p. 41). One simply takes his beliefs to be true because like everybody else he sees no reason to doubt them. This type of inferring is quite group-like. It leads to a store house of tried and true beliefs.

> They give us in great measure our morality, our politics, our social code, our art of life. They supply the elements of public opinion, the watchwords of patriotism, the standards of thought and action; they are our mutual understandings, our channels of sympathy, our means of co-operation, and the bond of our civil union. They become our moral language; we learn them as we learn our mother tongue; they distinguish us from foreigners; *they are, in each of us, not indeed personal, but national characteristics.* [my italics] (p. 42)

We should not be too quick to condemn this type of assent because it stems from our nature as social animals. If we react as Descartes did, we would disown our dependence on society. But the fact that we are still alive attests to the fact that our parents and ancestors must have taught us something right. The dinosaurs are extinct. We are still kicking.

Those who give credence to a proposition have no difficulty admitting they are believers. Information pours in upon everyone from all sides and is accepted as true unless there is some obvious reason to doubt it. For example, school children assent to what they have been taught by their teachers. There is nothing unnatural here. It is a virtue that the young be open to the teachings of their elders. College students harvest a great deal of information and imbibe a host of notions that constitute, as Newman says, "the furniture" of a gentleman's mind. Such knowledge enables us to relate more intelligently to our own concerns and those of society in general. Nevertheless, these notions are still abstractions. As such, they lack the passion and root of real assent.

Real Assent

In contrast, Newman gives an example drawn from religion to dramatize the difference between the notional assent of credence and real assent.

> Theology, as such, always is notional, as being scientific: religion, as being personal, should be real; but, except within a small range of subjects, it commonly is not real in England. As to Catholic populations, such as those of medieval Europe, or the Spain of this day, or quasi-Catholic as those of Russia, among them assent to religious objects is real, not notional. (p. 42)

The former is belief in the truth of a notion and the latter is belief in the truth about a particular thing or person. He characterizes as notional the assent given by the majority of the Englishmen in his day to the tenets of religion. They took for granted the truths of the creed in which they had been raised, respecting but not thinking about them very much. The beliefs were part of the general culture. Newman contrasts this attitude with the religion of people in the Middle Ages or in the Spain or Russia of his day. Here their belief is in actual persons--Christ, his Mother and the Saints—and in actual places. Heaven and Hell are more real to them than the houses they live in. Saints are not mere pictures on a wall; they are present in the house. In Newman's view, the only belief to which most religious Englishmen of the day gave real assent to was God's Providence over the nation, a lesson they learned from the devout and regular way they had been taught to read the Bible and from the historical lore of how God saved England from those Papists sailing in the Spanish Armada.

Credence certainly has its place in the education of the young. Because of the real assent they give to the word of respected elders, they hold many propositions to be true without comprehending them. In the course of time, propositions learned in the catechism take on more meaning as the doctrines take on more life in the celebrations of the liturgy and popular devotions. Though unseen, divine persons and places bind the minds and imaginations of believers in a way impossible to general theological notions. The way these beliefs are transmitted is by the hearts and minds of Bishops touching the hearts and minds of priests who in turn transmit to the hearts and minds of their people the reality of unseen persons. In turn are the parents raising their children. A child cannot help but be impressed by fathers and mothers who say their prayers and go to church, not because everybody else does, but because they have the proper fear and love of Christ, his Mother, and the Saints.

3) Opinion (p. 44)

Although the notional assents or beliefs of profession and credence stand on their own, they have been preceded by reasoning that is largely based on what society holds. We will now consider a type of assent which follows when a person matures. It is based upon what the individual has come to hold by his own efforts. After noting that the term "opinion" is used in different ways, Newman gives his own way of using it.

> I shall here use the word to denote an assent, but an assent to a proposition, not as true, but as probably true, that is, *to the probability of that which the proposition enunciates*; [my italics] and, as that probability may vary in strength without limit, so may the cogency and moment of the opinion. (p. 45)

Unlike profession and credence, opinion is the result of a more deliberate act of the mind assenting to the probability of a proposition being true. In profession and credence, one accepts the truth of a proposition unconditionally without much thought. Assenting to a proposition as probable is a more deliberate act, a sign of intellectual maturity. As children, we believed Santa Clause to be a real person or our parents and teachers to be infallible. With more experience of life, we put those beliefs aside and took a more reasonable position, thus leaving the poetry of youth for the prose of age. The process is natural.

Next, he distinguishes between a proposition expressing assent to a probability and a proposition which is a probable conclusion. Here we have a very subtle distinction. The statement "I am of the opinion that we shall have a fine hay-harvest this year" (p. 45) is to give assent to the probability of an outcome. Although the speaker could appeal to premises to justify his statement, he does not do so. He simply assents to a probable truth. In contrast is the speaker who says: "We shall have a fine hay-harvest if the present weather lasts." The claim of having a fine harvest is an inference drawn from the premise "if the fine weather lasts". The difference between assenting to a probability and inferring one is that the former stands on its own while the latter does not.

Religious Opinions

But Newman is far more interested in opinions about religion than in those about the weather. In the proposition "I believe in God" the believer assents to the existence of God as a truth. A truth excludes a non-truth. Consequently, the proposition that God does not exist is held to be false. The believer is not claiming the ability to prove it. Still, he holds that the atheist is wrong. Now consider the proposition "I am of the opinion that God exists." Here we have assent to a probability. A probability does not absolutely exclude its contrary. Therefore, the possibility that God does not exist remains in view. Over the years, Newman recognized the decline in English society from credence to opinion on this important proposition. A people having the belief that God exists hold that atheists are wrong. Believers have taken a stand. A people holding merely the opinion that God exists allow for a wide variety of opinion. The cultural atmosphere is looser.

So Far

So far, Newman has examined three types of notional assent. Profession is belief in what is taken to be the truth of a notion about such matters as party affiliation or fashion. It has the least intellectual weight because the inference preceding it is without much thought. The way leading to credence is to believe in the truth of notions that have been handed down as part of the culture. It has more intellectual weight than profession because it accords with general views. The way leading to an opinion is more deliberate. It is to assent to the truth of a proposition expressing the probable truth of a notion.

Deliberate Notional Assents

In the following two sections, Newman examines the notional assents of the highest order because they follow after efforts of 1) pure intellection and 2) demonstration. Here, Newman will be following the path laid down by Aristotle. Aristotle starts with the fact that all knowledge begins with experience of individual bodies through the senses. From this experience Aristotle induces (arrives at) the definitions or notions of four kinds of bodies. There are inorganic bodies like rocks studied in physics, organic bodies like plants studied in botany, organic bodies with senses studied in zoology, and rational animals studied in psychology. These investigators do not have to prove that these bodies exist. They see them. Seeing them, they are then able to define them. Thus, the definitions of the various kinds of bodies serve as the intellectual starting points or first principles of the sciences in question. There are as many of these as there are sciences. Here's how Newman expresses it.

4) Presumption (p. 45)

> *By presumption I mean an assent to first principles and by first principles I mean the propositions with which we start in reasoning about any given subject matter.* [my italics] They are in consequence very numerous and vary in great measure with the person who reasons, according to their judgment and power of assent, being received by some minds, not by others, and only a few of

> them received universally. *They are all of them notions, not images, because they express what is abstract, not what is individual and from direct experience.* [italics mine] (p.45)

Because there are many subject matters, there are many starting points or first principles. Because people vary in the depth of their experience of things, they vary in their acceptance of first principles. They are received by some and rejected by others. For example, those who specialize in the study of non-living bodies have a tendency to explain all bodies in terms of inorganic first principles. They do not take into account that plants, animals, or men have different first principles because they are living bodies.

Universal First Principles

Besides the first principles that each science has, there are first principles which apply to all subject matters. They should be accepted by everyone. He then gives an example of what should not be taken as a first principle:

> Sometimes our trust in our powers of reasoning and memory, that is, our implicit assent to their telling truly, is treated as a first principle; but we cannot properly be said to have any trust in them as faculties. (p. 46)

Without saying so, he is rejecting the stand of Descartes. As we saw, Descartes started by doubting the worth of sense knowledge and then undertook a long demonstration to show finally that the senses were trustworthy. Newman rejects the trustworthiness of the senses as a first principle, saying:

> At most we trust in *particular* [my italics] acts of memory and reasoning. We are sure there was a yesterday, and that we did this or that in it; we are sure that three times six is eighteen, and that the diagonal of a square is longer than the side. So far as this we may be said to trust the mental act, by which the object of our assent is verified; but, in doing so, we imply no

recognition of a general power or faculty, or of any capability or affection of our minds, over and above the particular act. (p. 46)

Newman insists on the primacy of a particular act of sense knowledge over mere trust in the powers of sensation. An old man may remember quite well what he did yesterday when, let us suppose, he went to town and did some shopping. Even if he is getting old and forgetful, he can still be certain of these particular events when questioned by someone. While he may in the past have been dreaming, drunk, or drugged, he knows that yesterday he was definitely awake, sober, and drug free. He had a good day. Similarly, in the case of the abstraction that six times three is eighteen, he knows it for certain even though he may be a poor mathematician. On this particular point he will be right even though he has failed tests in mathematics all his life. It is the awareness of the particular act of assenting to the truth of a fact or notion that gives man certainty, not some general trust in his powers of sense, memory, or intellect.

Newman brings up another truth known by reflection. He says:

> We know indeed that we have a faculty by which we remember, as we know we have a faculty by which we breathe; but *we gain this knowledge by abstraction or inference from its particular acts, not by direct experience.* [my italics] Nor do we trust in the faculty of memory or reasoning as such, even after that we have inferred its existence; for its acts are often inaccurate, nor do we invariably assent to them. (p. 46)

Newman is taking a page right out of Aristotle. Our direct knowledge is only of the acts of seeing, hearing, smelling, or feeling things that are colored, sounding, smelly, or textured. We have our knowledge directly from the acts whereby we sense things. We can be certain about them. From this experience of basic facts, we can, like Aristotle, infer that we have the powers that enable us to perform these acts. We can then infer that among these powers is the faculty of memory because we can recall our past acts. By no means, however, do we place our trust in any of these powers as such. We can make mistakes in their use. But we will not be mistaken about, for example, the particular fact that we went to town yesterday to do some shopping or that six times three is eighteen.

Special Note

Note especially that the certitude we have about the first principle that the world exists does not come from its being just in the intellect. No. The general principle is in the intellect only because of the knowledge of individual bodies in the senses. Without this knowledge, there is no first principle in the intellect. Furthermore, it is important to note that before acts of sense apprehension take place, the sense powers and intellect are utter blanks, "tabula rasas" as Aristotle says. The sense powers are not like empty forms waiting for the material of sense experience to be poured into them like concrete poured into pre-existing forms. No. Rather the senses pick up on the fact that bodies are formed because bodies in the world already have forms. If we do not take this position, we fall into the fallacy that the senses do not pick up on the way individual bodies exist in themselves but only impose their own forms on the raw material coming into them. No, no, no. That's the mistake Descartes and most modern philosophers made, thereby creating a gap between sense experience and individual bodies as they exist in themselves. From that mistake much mischief has followed. It is sense knowledge that forms the basis from which the first principle that bodies exist is formed. It is not the first principle that dictates the form our sense experience takes.

A Related Reason

Newman offers another reason for rejecting as a first principle trust in one's memory or reasoning powers. "It seems to me unphilosophical to speak of trusting ourselves. We are what we are and we use, not trust, our faculties." (p.

46) Having been born into a world we did not make, we take the world as we find it. We have no choice. It is what it is whether we like it or not. Now we are composites of body and mind. We first see, hear, smell, and touch things and then go on from there to fashion the various sciences about them. Descartes refuses to go that way. He withholds assent to the truth of the act of sensing a thing until he arrives at assent to the truth that he exists. While that assent is certainly true, he still has the task of creating a long train of inferences to get back to the real world. For the awareness he has of himself is the self of a pure mind, an intellect that is not connected with a body. To get his body back again, he has to undertake a long demonstration proving that he can trust his sense powers. But, as Newman points out, it is unreal to place trust in sense powers. They can be mistaken. It is the memory of a particular act of sensing that grounds our assent to the first principle that the world of bodies exists. No proof is needed. My certainty that I have a computer before me contains implicitly the first principle that there is a world out there.

The moral of the story is that if you doubt the truth of the acts of sensation which make you identical cognitively with your companion at the dinner table, you have cut yourself off from the real world and will not get back to it again. A long demonstration connecting the knowledge of yourself as a thinking thing that finally reasons its way to being connected with a body will not do the job. Like a balloon, you will float up into the sky of abstractions and never come down again—unless, of course, some kindly friend puts a needle into your balloon and pops it. The result will be a hard landing. But such a landing is better than no landing at all.

Universal Principle

What is the universal principle covering all subject matters to which everybody should consider to be obviously and certainly true? Newman answers that it is the universal principle that the world of material bodies exists. This principle is implicitly known by everyone in every act of sensing the bodies around them. Technically speaking, this generalization is the result of an induction, not a demonstration. An induction moves from particular facts right up to general principles. In realist epistemology, the starting point are bodily things existing as individuals in themselves. Sense knowledge is the result. This result is expressed in the generalization that the world exists. This principle anchors intellectually the definitions of things like rocks, trees, animals, or men. The definitions of these form the first principles of the sciences in question. Demonstrations or inferences follow from them. If, however, the connection of man's knowledge of things with things themselves is broken, demonstrations will be just about ideas in the mind. We will have become ideologues—students of ideas—not students of things.

The Moral Order

Since Newman has set out to examine first principles in general, he has to go on to treat the first principles of the moral order for the sake of being complete. There is right and wrong. As in the case of sense knowledge where man is a blank before he actually senses things, so in the case of moral knowledge man is a blank before he learns right from wrong. But as a child reaches the age of reason when he sees particular deeds of kindness or of cruelty, he knows without argument that kindness is right and cruelty is wrong. In a fit of passion, he might whack his brother over the head with a hammer. He has done a cruel deed. But if vigorously corrected, he will see that he is wrong. A bit later in keeping with his intellectual development, he judges a man who gives up his life for another as a hero and a man who goes about raping and pillaging as a criminal. These particular judgments already move on the presumption that there is right and wrong. If one wishes to turn this presumption into a universal first principle, he abstracts from all particular circumstances and states that there is right and wrong in general.

The Foundation

The foundation for a philosophical realist is the same in the order of both knowledge and morality. That foundation is man as a composite or unit of body and soul comes into the world as a blank tablet. Through the activity of the senses, he becomes one with things. Having become one with things, he is able to abstract, to draw first principles from them. His definitions give him the essential nature of the things and their operations. In the moral order, the movement is the same. With time, he experiences particular acts of kindness or cruelty by suffering or doing them. Implicit in this sense is a grasp of right and wrong. Further reflection reveals the first principle that there is right and wrong in general. That's the way that men, not angels, learn how they should live their lives.

5) Speculation (p. 54)

We now come to the last type of notional assent, which Newman calls speculation. Like the other four types, a speculation is a proposition in the form of an assent given to the truth of a notion. Unlike the other four types, it is preceded by demonstrative inference, the most perfect type there is. This type covers mathematical demonstrations, the determinations of science and the doctrines of theology. He says:

> That there is a God, that He has certain attributes, and in what sense He can be said to have attributes, that He has done certain works, that He has made certain revelations of Himself and of His will, and what they are, and the multiplied bearings of the parts of the teaching, thus developed and formed, upon each other, all this is the subject of notional assent, and of that particular department of it which I have called Speculation. *As far as these particular subjects can be viewed in the concrete and represent experiences, they can be received by real assent also; but as expressed in general propositions they belong to notional apprehension and*

assent. [my italics] (p. 54)

Let us consider the theological demonstration concluding "Therefore God exists." The conclusion is conditional in the sense that its truth depends on premises. Since the premises in this type of demonstration are certainly true, the conclusion is certainly true. Note that the conclusion is still an inference, the result of an argument. It only becomes an assent when the proposition takes the unqualified form: "God exists." This proposition leaves aside the argumentative form and becomes an assertion of a truth. The assent is notional. This proposition, however, can become a real assent should one say: "I kneel down and ask forgiveness from my Lord and Savior." Here is an act of religion that puts believers on their knees in acts of adoration and gratitude. The act is personal. (Newman will amplify on this point in Chapter Five of the *Essay*.)

Step of the Argument

In order to set up a contrast between notional and real assent, Newman describes five types of propositions expressing notional assent—profession, credence, opinion, presumption, and speculation. Since they deal with what is taken to be the truth of notions, they reside in the intellect, not the imagination. Thus, they do not influence our actions as powerfully as real assents do.

Chapter Eight

Notional and Real Assent (Second Part of Chapter Four of the *Essay*)

Since notional assents reside in the intellect, they do not move us as powerfully as real assents, which have their home in the imagination. Newman begins with his account of real assent.

> I have in a measure anticipated the subject of Real Assent by what I have been saying about Notional. In comparison of the directness and force of the apprehension, which we have of an object, when our assent is to be called real, Notional Assent and Inference seem to be thrown back into one and the same class of intellectual acts, though the former of the two is always an unconditional acceptance of a proposition, and the latter is an acceptance on the condition of an acceptance of its premises. *In its notional assents as well as in its inferences, the mind contemplates its own creations instead of things*; [italics mine] in real, it is directed towards things, represented by the impressions which they have left on the imagination. These images, when assented to, have an influence both on the individual and on society, which mere notions cannot exert. (p. 55)

Notional assent and inference are creations of the mind. If there were no minds, obviously there would not be the activities of assenting or of inferring. Neither would there be the imagination's activity of creating images. There is, however, a tremendous difference between philosophical realists and philosophical idealists in regard to the images in the mind. Realists take for granted that the images formed are naturally caused by bodies in the world. Still, there may be exceptions because the sense organs may be disturbed. A drunk may see pink elephants or one on LSD see snakes. But with more experience of life these aberrations may be judged as such. In contrast, idealists cast doubt on the natural connection between images in their mind and bodies causing them. But, instead of relying on more experience to correct their impressions, a Cartesian will leave the sensible world and rely on the intellect alone. They will resort to detached reasoning rather than relying on more experience with bodies in the world.

In doing so, they change the standard of truth. For the realist, the standard of truth of whether a tree is on a lawn or not is determined finally by whether the tree is there or not. If it is there, those who say it is not there are wrong, case closed. The idealist has no such standard because he has put in doubt the fact that the tree is there. Consequently, he will place the standard of truth in his philosophical reasoning, not ordinary experience. His reason sees two possibilities. The first is that the images are caused by outside bodies. The second is that the images are caused by aberrations in the sense organs.

Consequently, he must enter into a full philosophical investigation concerning whether he can trust his senses or not. The result is the reign of the subjective and the decline of the objective when it comes to making judgments about the real world. Idealists find themselves each living in their own private world. They have no outside reference point. Realists have things in the world as the standard or corrective. Newman admits that the vividness of an impression is no guarantee that the impression is true. In the final analysis, the matter of whether a tree on a lawn is really there or not depends on our ability to know the tree is there whether we like it or not. The idealist makes the fatal move of undercutting that ability, thus reducing all sense knowledge to a knowledge of what at best only a probability.

Keeping these remarks in mind, let us observe how Newman describes the transition from notional assent to real assent. He considers such a transition to be natural, meaning that the more experience people have of life, the more realization they have of what they are talking about. They move from an abstract hold on reality to a real grasp of it.

Transitions

Newman now proceeds to give examples of transitions from notional to real assent based on nature's pattern. We move from the notional assents which are the beliefs fostered by society (profession and credence), on through the notional assents of probability (opinion), until the educated arrive at the highest notional assents of all, presumption and speculation. Because they are notional, they reside in the intellect, not in the imagination. Hence they inform us intellectually, not move us emotionally. With more experience of the world, however, we are increasingly gripped by things. We move from a notional assent to a truth to a real assent we take to be a living truth. Newman gives many examples of this normal transition.

> For instance: boys at school look like each other, and pursue the same studies, some of them with greater success than others; but it will sometimes happen, that those who acquitted themselves but poorly in class, when they come into the action of life, and engage in some particular work, which they have already been learning in its theory and with little promise of proficiency, are suddenly found to have what is called an eye for that work—an eye for trade matters, or for engineering, or a special taste for literature—which no one expected from them at school, while they were engaged on notions. (p. 55)

There is be more that goes on in a student than learning notions at school. Take, for example, a seminary classroom. There are some who have grown up with a special talent for sympathizing with others. But the setting in a seminary classroom does not allow much for the exhibition of such a talent. It is only after they graduate and enter their ministries that they show great success in dealing with their congregations. It seems as if they were born to deal with the joys and sorrows of individuals and families. No one would have expected it of them, least of all themselves. Newman continues:

> Minds of this stamp not only know the received rules of their profession, but enter into them, and even anticipate them, or dispense with them, or substitute other rules instead. And when new questions are opened, and arguments are drawn up on one side and the other in long array, they with a natural ease and promptness form their views and give their decision, as if they had no need to reason, from their clear apprehension of the lie and issue of the whole matter in dispute, as if it were drawn out in a map before them. These are the reformers, systematizers, inventors, in various departments of thought, speculative and practical; in education, in administration, in social and political matters, in science. (p. 55)

Newman adds a cautionary note:

> Such men indeed are far from infallible; however great their powers, they sometimes fall into great errors, in their own special department, while second-rate men who go by rule come to sound and safe conclusions. Images need not be true; but I am illustrating what vividness of apprehension is, and what is the strength of belief consequent upon it. (p.55)

Formal schooling is for the most part notional. It provides the young with the intellectual framework they will fill in as they gain more experience of life. But there are some students who do not fit this pattern. They show poorly in recitations and are bored with abstractions. But when they enter the world, they show amazing insight into what is going on. They know how to act as if they had an internal map that makes them great successes in their chosen fields. They have a real apprehension of things firing their imaginations. They get things done and are able to influence others to follow them. Nevertheless, they are not infallible. While they do not make routine mistakes in their field, they may make big mistakes that less daring and second-rate people would never make. They may not be right. But they are always effective.

Uncanny

The fact that some individuals have an uncanny ability to deal with concrete matters is explained by the fact sense knowledge of particular things provides man's entrance into reality. There is no other way. Now things not only have a nature from which characteristic operations flow, thus making them objects of science. But they are also bodies interacting with each other in all kinds of surprising ways. These ways are accidental to their nature. For example, a mountain goat accidentally dislodges a few rocks which start an avalanche which wipes out a citadel which was necessary for a defense of a nation, thus leaving it helpless before the hordes of enemies who eventually pour in. As improbable as this scenario is, it could have the merit of actually happening. It could be that the misstep of a goat caused the fall of a nation. Knowing the ways of goats and hillsides, an old mountaineer might have had a sense that such could happen. But who would ever listen to him? Reality is full of surprises. It escapes the ken of philosophers and scientists who, focusing quite rightly on the necessities entailed in the nature of things, overlook their accidental possibilities. They have to overlook these possibilities because they are indefinite in scope. But sometimes they actually happen!

Another Example

Newman gives another example, this time of the passage in a nation from notional to real assent. After the Duke of Wellington defeated Napoleon at Waterloo, he laid out a program that the nation should adopt in order to have an adequate defense. The public accepted these suggestions on the authority of the great hero but did not do anything about them for thirty years. Only when a new crisis presented itself did the reforms suggested by the Duke become objects of real assent. There was no change in the beliefs of the public. The change consisted in the way those beliefs were apprehended.

The Practice of Meditation

In another example, Newman cites the Catholic practice of meditating on the mysteries portrayed in the Gospels, the result being a transition from notional assent to real assent. Here, the mysteries take on new life when the experience of the believer catches up with the mystery portrayed in the sacred account. What was just a story, even a sacred one, now grabs his imagination. An experience in his or her life opens up the mystery upon which one meditates. In another example, he speaks of a preacher who, through long practice, has disclaimed for many years on the crucifixion of Christ as if it were a mere notion that he had to work up so to impress his congregation. But at a certain point, his heart may be ploughed by grief. It is then that the Gospel account becomes real. It is then that the preacher's heart warms the congregation's heart. The man is no longer exhibiting his powers of persuasion. He has gotten down from his pulpit and joined his people in their joys and sorrows. The hope he imparts is real.

The Movers of Society

We should not think that because real apprehension of beliefs gives reformers, systematizers, inventors, etc., a special energy in pursuing their projects that they are necessarily right. What they hold to be true may really be illusions. But these illusions will be pushed with great energy, thus, driving truths that are only notionally apprehended off the public stage. There is the possibility, then, of a whole culture being dominated by unbelief as a driving force shaping the imaginations and hearts of men as completely as the culture of religious belief once shaped Western Man.

The Key Feature

The key feature of real assent or belief is that it supplies the drive to man's life for better or for worse. The phenomena of notional assent explain how the beliefs of a society are able to be passed down from one generation to another. General statements are notional and, therefore, communicable. They can be put into words. They can be expressed by elders and received by the inexperienced as truths. They provide a general framework. But it is each person's real assents or beliefs that put the fire into him or her that ignites the fire in others for either a worthy or an unworthy cause.

Section Three: Notional and Real Assents Contrasted

Newman summarizes:

> However, on the whole, broadly contrasting Belief with Notional Assent and with Inference, we shall not, with this explanation, be very wrong in pronouncing that acts of Notional Assent and of Inference do not affect our conduct, and acts of Belief, that is, of Real Assent, do (not necessarily, but do) affect it. (p. 64)

Note Well

It is important to note that giving real assent to the truth of a thing is no guarantee that you have the truth about the way things really are. While Descartes was wrong in giving real assent to the proposition that the senses are unreliable, he nevertheless found enough support in the hearts and minds of influential thinkers so that in the present day distrust of sense knowledge is typical. The disease is real. It is immune to the argument of philosophers dedicated to being realistic. Like a plague, it has a power of its own.

An Earlier Piece

We now come to the selection with which Newman concludes Chapter Four, itself a development of the three previous chapters. Let us analyze this selection because it brings into focus the whole argument up to this point. Previously, we have been like bystanders observing a chess master setting up the pieces of his argument. We have seen each of his moves in defining the basic terms and filling them in with examples from the ordinary experience of life without knowing quite where he is going. Where he is going is to finally call "checkmate" on his opponents.

He begins by quoting twenty-nine years later a large section of a piece he had written in 1841, four years before he became a Catholic. He begins by noting that the statesmen of his day were mounting a campaign to improve the morals of society, especially the lower classes. In the past, the improvement of morals was connected with direct instruction in Christian doctrine. Modern statesmen now have other ideas. Newman analyzes the doctrine that animates them:

> That doctrine was to the effect that the claims of religion could be secured and sustained in the mass of men, and in particular in the lower classes of society, by acquaintance with literature and physical science, and through the instrumentality of Mechanics' Institutes and Reading Rooms, to the serious disparagement, as it seemed to me, of direct Christian instruction. (p. 65)

Exercises of inference are to take the place of believing. This description of society in the 1840's is in seed form his description of society in the 1870's; it is headed for an apocalypse of unbelief. Later on, politicians will not bother with connecting the improvement of society by making a pious bow to Christianity. But in the 1840's, Christianity was still enough of a cultural presence to require at least a bow. Somehow, the availability of Mechanics' Institutes and Reading Rooms, not instruction in the catechism, will make people more moral in an age when Christianity is losing its social effectiveness.

Today

Catholics have seen the same kinds of change in the late 1960's and 1970's. The Baltimore Catechism, which had shaped the faith of American Catholics since 1885, was put aside as too abstract, too definite about basic doctrines, too clear about the reality of Heaven, Purgatory, and Hell, and altogether too hard on Protestants. The catechism not only gave the answers to be given. It set the questions to be asked. Most terrible of all to modernists, it had little boys and girls memorizing its articles and then being graded on their success.

In brief, it would seem that the vast majority of bishops and lay people trained in the catechism and in St. Thomas Aquinas had the right stamp. But as the 1960's unrolled, it became clear that they collapsed in the face of new experts extolling the virtues of "The Spirit of Vatican Two". After that period, instruction in the catechism declined with the result in later generations of abysmal ignorance. The point is that notional assents even to truths cannot hold their own on the public stage against the power of real assents given to illusions.

Newman Continues

> People say to me, that it is but a dream to suppose that Christianity should regain the organic power in human society that once it possessed. I cannot help that; I never said it could. I am not a politician; I am proposing no measures, but exposing a fallacy and resisting a pretense. . . .Do not attempt by philosophy what was once done by religion. The ascendancy of faith may be impractical, but

the reign of knowledge is incomprehensible. The problem for the statesmen of this age is how to educate the masses, and literature and science cannot give the solution. (p. 65)

Newman brushes off any accusation that he is trying to turn back the clock by urging a program that will restore Christianity to the role it once had in English society for over a thousand years. He is no politician. Rather, he is puncturing the great balloon of an illusion that mere reasoning has the power to change the morals of a people. The pride and passion of man is not so easily tamed. Here he speaks in the same way he had been speaking during his analysis or ordinary human experience in the first four chapters of his *Essay*. He simply describes the way human beings assent and infer without any effort to distinguish the right from the wrong way to do so. On that basis, he judges the program of the statesmen to be simply unreal, a theory that cannot bear up when the facts of life are taken into consideration.

Describing this theory, he says:

> Science gives us the grounds or premises from which religious truths are to be inferred; but it does not set about inferring them, much less does it reach the inference—that is not its province. It brings before us phenomena, and it leaves us, if we will, to call them works of design, wisdom, or benevolence; and further still, if we will, to proceed to confess an Intelligent Creator. We have to take in its facts, and to give them a meaning, and to draw our own conclusions from them. *First comes knowledge, then a view, then reasoning, then belief.* [my italics] That is why science has so little of religious tendency; deductions have so little a power of persuasion. (p. 65)

In the theory advocated by the statesmen of the 1840's, scientific reason comes first and religious belief comes later. Scientific reason does its work of showing the laws explaining the order in nature. In a culture which still considered itself to be Christian by way of credence, people were inclined to interpret this order as the work of an intelligent Creator. But a later age influenced by Darwin, who explained that order into terms of an evolutionary process using natural selection as the cause, not any Deity, became the fashion. The point is that scientific facts can be interpreted either way. Now, even if one holds that the facts indicate a Deity as the cause, the inference is still notional. It does not involve the imagination where religious belief has the power to move us.

Newman goes on to give us the central image driving his philosophizing:

> The heart is commonly reached, not through the reason, but through the imagination by means of direct impressions, by the testimony of facts and events, by history, by description. Persons influence us, voices melt us, looks subdue us, deeds inflame us. Many a man will live and die upon a dogma; no man will be a martyr for a conclusion. A conclusion is but an opinion; it is not a thing which is; but which we are 'quite sure about'. (p. 65)

And there we have everything summed up! It explains why my parents from the West of Ireland imprinted me so deeply with The Faith. I loved them because they were good to me. It also explains why many in my generation began to lose their grip on The Faith. Being prosperous and successful in a new land took the edge off The Faith their ancestors had bequeathed them. In general, prosperity is not conducive to being religious in a deep way. We grow too soft in waging the war against the world, the flesh, and the devil.

Newman's view of the power of persons to impress us also explains the loss of The Faith. The practice of The Faith entails a tension between the knowledge of what we should do and our desire to do the opposite. To the obligation to be chaste and sober, there is the desire to do what we wish in matters of sex and drink. The war is long and hard. In the midst of it, people are tempted to give up. Some do give up. But instead of quietly indulging themselves, they rise up in rage and resentment at a religion they see as authoritarian, rigid, repressive, unnatural, and the rest in favor of a creed which is egalitarian, flexible, liberating, and natural. With the fire they have in themselves, they light the fire in others.

The Impossibility

Newman goes on to show the impossibility of a religion of inferences:

> Life is not long enough for a religion of inferences; we shall never have done beginning, if we determine to begin with proof. We shall ever be laying our foundations; we shall turn theology into evidences, and divines into textuaries. We shall never get at our first principles. Resolve to believe nothing, and you must prove your proofs and analyze your elements, sinking farther and farther, and finding 'in the lowest depth a lower deep', till you come to the broad bosom of skepticism. (p. 67)

Here is a perfect description of what happens to one who subjects his belief to an intellectual inquiry. Let us suppose that a Catholic is in doubt whether Christ founded the Catholic Church or not. In posing the question in this manner, he has done what he should not do as a Catholic. He has laid aside his belief that Christ did indeed found the Catholic Church. He has sinned mortally because he has chosen to open his mind to other possibilities. He begins a reading program that includes religious and non-religious thinkers. He also has to check the various commentaries on the Bible and review problems in Church History. How many years will it take him to reach a conclusion? And what will his conclusion be? At best it will be the probability that Christ founded the Church. But belief even in a high probability is not the same as belief in a definite truth. It is but an opinion. Belief in the probability of Christ's being the

Good Shepherd does not make our inquirer a sheep in the flock. He will still be an outsider. Everything religious will be but a matter of opinion. The practice of religion will be a kind of formalism. Outwardly, he may trot along with the rest of the sheep but inwardly reserve to himself the right to pick and choose his particular way.

An Ordinary Life Based on Inference

This argument showing the impossibility of a religion based on inference can be applied to the impossibility of ordinary life being lived on inferences. Suppose one doubts the connection between the images and notions in his mind and individual things outside it. Once you do that, you will never be able to make the connection, to build a bridge between the two. There is nothing in the experience of ideas or images in your mind that will force you to say that they are caused by things outside it. For you are faced with two possibilities. The first is that the image within is caused by the thing without. The second is that the image within is caused by the mind itself, as is the case with dreamers and drunks. Weighing the two possibilities will not provide a solution. For experience shows that nightmares can be tremendously vivid, and looking at things in the light of day can bore us. The result is that we can have no absolute certitude about our sense knowledge of bodies. We can only have the belief, not the knowledge, that elephants are gray, not pink, that sticks placed in the water are still straight, not bent, or that water appearing on a desert road is a mirage, not real. The only solution is to go the natural way of admitting that we can tell the difference between seeing something in real life and seeing something in our dreams. We go with the human condition although sometimes we may not want to do so.

Anti-Intellectual in Attitude?

To ward off the objection that he is being anti-intellectual, Newman goes on to say:

> *I only say, that impressions lead to action, and that*

reasonings lead from it. [my italics] Knowledge of premises and inferences from them, this is not to live. *It is very well as a matter of liberal curiosity and of philosophy to analyze our modes of thought: but let this come second, and when there is leisure for it, and then our examination will in many ways even be subservient to action.* [my italics] But if we commence with scientific knowledge and argumentative proof, or lay any great stress upon it as the basis of personal Christianity, or attempt to make man moral and religious by libraries and museums, let us in consistency take chemists for our cooks, and mineralogists for our masons. (p. 67)

No Opponent

Newman is no opponent of liberal studies or philosophy-- when they are kept in their proper place. That place is within the larger context of living a life. We are born without our consent. We find ourselves with parents who care for and educate us in the way they think best. We find ourselves in a city or nation that we have not designed. It has its own traditions, its way of looking at life. In the process we begin to live our own lives equipped with the real assents or beliefs that we have been led to make, whether those beliefs are sound or unsound. The notion that the formally educated are the most reliable judges of what is real is simply unreal. And yet this fat balloon of an illusion can prevail as if it were the most obvious of truths. It can dominate a culture. But even such a culture has enough good sense left not to take chemists for its cooks or mineralogists for its masons. But when it comes to religion, this is what modern people do. Using the ways of formal inference, modern philosophers begin to chip away at common sense and religious faith, holding them to be simple-minded or naïve or blind, fit for children but not for adults.

Religion In General

Newman, applying his stand concerning real assent or real belief to religion in general, says

> that no religion yet has been a religion of physics or of philosophy. It has ever been synonymous with revelation. It never has been a deduction from what we know; it has ever been an assertion of what we are to believe. It has never lived in a conclusion; it has ever been a message, a history, or a vision. No legislator or priest ever dreamed of educating our moral nature by science or by argument. There is no difference here between true religion and pretended. Moses was instructed not to reason from the creation, but to work miracles. Christianity is a history supernatural, and almost scenic: it tells us what its Author is, by telling us what He has done ...(p.68)

Newman is speaking of religion as it has shown itself in the history of mankind. It is something revealed, a message, a story, a vision from a higher source. It comes with authority. The message is that we are to live our lives on earth in fear and trembling of being unjust, impure, greedy, contentious. We need the guidance of religious authority to keep us on the straight and narrow. I would add that political authorities do not entrust themselves to the persuasion of mere argument. They make laws that are backed up by force. If you break them, you are fined, imprisoned, or even executed.

Newman Thrusts

At the end of his piece, Newman slips his dagger in between the ribs of his opponents, saying:

> Lord Broughan [one of the political figures behind the social program] has recognized the force of this principle [the power of real assent]. He has not left his philosophical religion to argument; he has committed it to the keeping of imagination. Why should he depict a great republic of letters, and an intellectual pantheon, except that he feels instances and patterns, not logical reasonings, are the living conclusions which alone have a hold over the affections or can form the character? (p. 68)

In this paragraph Newman brings to a head his whole argument. His opponents have argued that scientific inference can do what real assent to religious propositions once did in maintaining the moral tone of society. But they do not bother with arguing with the public. Instead, they create monuments to impress its imagination. They thereby confirm Newman's stand that for better or for worse it is real assent or belief, not inference, that shapes the character of individuals and the culture of communities.

Newman's point in this chapter also brings to a head the argument of the previous three chapters. His opponents have argued in effect that the changes in the character of individuals and the culture of communities is due to the power of scientific inference. The higher the probable truth of an inference is, the higher will its power be to improve society. They call this process progress. Newman calls it an apocalypse.

Conclusion

We may now draw a final conclusion from Newman's argument extending over four chapters. We are moved far more by beliefs based on the real apprehension of actual people or things than by conclusions drawn from the study of the sciences. Everybody starts out life as a believer trusting in the authority of his or her parents or of those who take their place. Belief in the word of authority sets the framework in which we apprehend the world in which we live. If, then, we are to explain any great change in the attitude of an individual or a community, we have look for a great change in their real beliefs. The explanation of moderns that the change from pre-scientific to modern times is because the sciences have taught us how to reason better is simply not true. The reality is that the images of what men love or hate have been undergoing a great change since the Sixteenth Century.

The monk Martin Luther started a revolution in how Catholics saw the Church. For sixteen centuries Catholics saw her as Christ's messenger. The Church was the flock, society or institution on earth leading to heaven. In contrast, Luther saw her as the Whore of Babylon led by the Pope, the Antichrist. The image of Holy Mother the Church had faded in the imagination of many baptized Catholics, the replacement being Protestants relying on Scriptures Alone. Thus began the conflict between two images deeply implanted in the imagination of Protestants and Catholics, a conflict that has continued to this day.

On an even deeper level we have seen how Descartes in the Seventeenth Century set the philosophical groundwork for images of man dominating nature rather than of man submitting to her. Formerly, man took for granted that his experience of bodily things in the world set the foundations for a search for their ultimate causes. After Descartes men increasingly took for granted that man alone is the cause that should be focused on. He starts to see himself as the Great Engineer taking the blueprints in his mind and imposing them on the raw material supplied by the world. The final result is the vision of man creating a heaven upon earth by the use of the modern sciences.

Step of the Argument

Chapter Four brings to a conclusion the argument of the first four chapters of the *Essay* concerning the relationship of assent to apprehension in matters of ordinary experience. The conclusion is that real assent or belief is the primary factor in forming the character of individuals and the culture of communities for better or for worse. Human beings start out in life as believers.

Chapter Nine

Assent and Apprehension in the Matter of Religion (Chapter Five of the *Essay*)

Newman now applies the lessons we have learned in the previous chapters to the matter of religion.

The First Paragraph

The first paragraph goes as follows:

> We are now able to determine what a dogma of faith is, and what it is to believe it. A dogma is a proposition; it stands for a notion or for a thing; and to believe it is to give the assent of the mind to it, as it stands for the one or for the other. To give a real assent to it is an act of religion; to give a notional, is a theological act. It is discerned, rested in, and appropriated as a reality, by the religious imagination; it is held as a truth, by the theological intellect. (p. 69)

We already understand many things about our Catholic faith because we practice it. But our understanding is implicit. Newman will make that understanding more explicit, more philosophical. Having laid the groundwork in ordinary matters, Newman declares that a dogma of faith is a proposition, a declarative sentence affirming a predicate of a subject unconditionally. It is not some vague inexpressible into which we can insert our own meaning. Consider the teachings of The Apostles' Creed. There is a real God who created this real world from nothing, that Jesus Christ is the only Son of the Father, was conceived of the Holy Spirit, was born of the Virgin Mary, suffered under Pontus Pilate, was crucified, and was buried. These events are real, concrete. They happened! Who says so? The Church speaking for God, says so. We should not be embarrassed because we are believers dependent upon authority. Being the way we accept the truth of ordinary matters, it is also the way of attaining the truth of supernatural matters. Consequently, it makes great sense that we give our unconditional assent to these propositions. People who disagree speak falsely. There is something quite simple, plain, and even fierce about dogmas. Assent to the truth of a person or thing (that Christ is to be worshiped, for example) is real assent, an act of religion. Assent to the truth of a notion (that there are Three Persons in One God, for example) is notional assent, a theological act.

There is continuity between the natural order we know by experience and the supernatural or revealed order we have learned by faith. Just as in the natural order, we hold many things as true because we trust in the word of our parents, teachers, and other authorities, so in the supernatural order we trust in the teachings of the Apostles, eyewitnesses to the words and life of Christ. In an apocalyptic age when ordinary and natural experience are put aside because of the age's enchantment with the illusion of building a heaven on earth, we can get confused, especially those of us in higher education. It is the institution that hands out the diplomas. In doing so, it has its own interests in mind, interests which have nothing to do either with those of the Catholic Church or of Western Civilization in general. It aims to be modern, up to date.

This confusion is quite understandable because we are social creatures who depend on our fellows for survival and information. When institutions make the choice of disowning the past in favor of some utopian future, we are in deep trouble. We breathe in this atmosphere as if it were life-giving air when it is really an anesthetic that numbs us to our natural life, let alone to our supernatural one. We have to start breathing real air.

Next Point

Newman now makes a connection between notional and real assent:

> Not as if there were in fact, or could be, any line of demarcation or party wall between these two modes of assent, the religious and the theological. As intellect is common to all men as well as imagination, every religious man is to a certain extent a theologian, and no theology can start or thrive without the initiative or abiding presence of religion. (p. 69)

Man is a single substance composed of body and soul that has the powers of sensing, imagining, and intellection. There is no wall separating these parts. The man who gives notional assent to the truth of a notion and real assent to the truth of a thing is the same man. But it takes time to put the apprehension of things together with the apprehension of notions in order to get some comprehension. Young adults in the university feed on the apprehension of notions by the bushel but it takes years of experience with things before they really know what they are talking about. So, too, in religious matters there is an intimate connection between the devotions of a religious man and the teachings of a theologian. Such devotions, for example, to the Sacred Heart or the Immaculate Conception, feed the imagination, grounding it in the religious facts. The teachings of the theologians in the catechism supply the explanation of the facts.

The last sixty years, however, have shown that as the devotions get lost, the catechism goes out the window. It is from a living faith that a sound theology arises. When the devotions languish, the articles of the catechism become empty and dry, thus leaving room for all sorts of heterodox opinions to thrive. The religious man must have a theology to guide his imagination while a theologian must have real belief inspiring his search for definitions. A religious man without theology has no safeguard against the abuses due to imagination. Superstition creeps in. A theologian without religion has no tether to save himself from floating off into the clouds and inventing his own religion. Heresy and apostasy are the result.

A Connection

What is the connection between Newman the philosophical realist emphasizing the importance of sense knowledge in knowing this world and Newman the Catholic in explaining the faith? He tells us:

> As in matters of this world, sense, sensation, instinct, intuition, supply us with facts and the intellect uses them, so, as regards out relations with the Supreme Being, we get our facts from the witness of nature, then of revelation, and our doctrines, in which they issue, through the exercise abstraction and inference. (p. 69)

He makes a comparison between ordinary knowledge and religious knowledge. In ordinary knowledge, we see, hear, smell or feel the things around us. We get an increasingly stronger grip on them by experience over time. The intellect then uses the facts to understand the nature of things and their causes. How does our belief in the Supreme Being fit into this scheme of knowledge? What are the facts open to any human being? First is the witness of nature. Creation itself witnesses to the existence of a Person to be worshipped. But because men are free, they can follow their nature or not, can either worship or not. Second is revelation. Those who choose to worship God will have the expectation that God will help them in a special way. They hope that God will reveal himself further than He has. Revelation adds to the natural truth of God's existence the supernatural truth revealed by Christ through his Church. Third, theologians who have given real assent to the basic facts of nature and revelation appropriate them by the tools of abstraction and inference. The result is a theology. The role of the theologian is similar to that of the philosopher. Just as the philosopher seeks to explain the facts known by ordinary experience in terms of their causes, the theologian seeks to explain what is known in the experience of saying our prayers, confessing our sins, going to mass, and obeying the Pope. Neither philosophers nor theologians are the inventors or creators of the facts. They do their best to explain what they have not made. They are spectators, contemplators, receivers of the truth about reality. It is their task to conform their minds to reality, not to shape reality according to their own desires.

A Clarification

Newman proceeds to clarify, saying:

> Now first, my subject is assent, and not inference. I am not proposing to set forth the arguments which issue in the belief of these doctrines, but to investigate what it is to believe in them, what the mind does, what it contemplates, when it makes an act of faith. (p. 69)

If his main concern had been with demonstrative inference, he would have been obliged to take on the metaphysician's role of demonstrating the existence of God. But his aim all along has been to be practical, thus avoiding excursions into pure metaphysics. Instead, he provides us with the vocabulary needed to articulate our basic experience as human beings in an atmosphere that threatens to make us forgetful of our humanity. Since his aim is practical, it would be out of place for him to go through all the steps a metaphysician would have to take to demonstrate the existence of God. In a practical argument, he can take for granted that Catholics believe in God.

Newman now comes to the key question:

> So far is clear [that dogmas may be the object of notional assent]; *but the question follows, Can I attain to any more vivid assent to the Being of a God, than that which is given merely to notions of the intellect? Can I enter*

> *with a personal knowledge into the circle of truths which make up that great thought? Can I rise to what I have called an imaginative apprehension of it? Can I believe as if I saw?* [my italics]. Since such a high assent requires a present experience or memory of the fact, at first sight it would seem as if the answer must be in the negative; for how can I assent as if I saw, unless I have seen? but no one in this life can see God. Yet I conceive that a real assent is possible, and I proceed to show how. (p. 71)

Newman proceeds to show that all men are capable of giving real assent to the concrete proposition that God is their Lord and Master. The reason is because by nature we are rational animals. We have the faculty of reason. Other animals don't. Possessing this faculty means that we are responsible for our actions. We have a conscience which tells us so through the feelings which it generates. The Good Samaritan helps the poor victim who has been waylaid by robbers. Thus he has the sense of having God's approval. Others pass the victim by either in indifference or with a slight, very slight, twinge of guilt. They have a sense, or at least should have, of God's disapproval. Such is the stuff of conscience. It is made of the feelings of either God's approval or disapproval for what we have done or failed to do.

Newman does not bother to debate the matter although he realizes that that the modern world despises this traditional view in the name of its own view of conscience. This view dictates that the secular project of creating a heaven on earth is the basic duty of any modern person, especially the educated. To intrude religious goals into this project is a violation of man's dignity. Does not mankind have the right to forge its own destiny after having endured centuries of prelates threatening them with the fires of hell if they do not obey the Church?

In this Chapter Five, Newman goes on to explain the traditional notion of conscience. But instead of following him, let me skip ahead to Chapter Ten where he picks up the

Assent and Apprehension in the Matter of Religion

subject of conscience again by starting with the notion of natural religion. My reason for skipping ahead is the very forceful way Newman deals with conscience, which means in Latin "acting with knowledge".

> By Religion I mean the knowledge of God, of His Will, and of our duties towards Him; and there are three main channels which Nature furnishes for our acquiring this knowledge, viz. our own minds, the voice of mankind, and the course of the world, that is, of human life and human affairs. The informations which these three convey to us teach us the Being and Attributes of God, our responsibility to Him, our dependence on Him, our prospect of reward or punishment, to be somehow brought about, according as we obey or disobey Him. And the most authoritative of these three means of knowledge, as being specially our own, is our own mind, whose informations give us the rule by which we test, interpret, and correct what is presented to us for belief, whether by the universal testimony of mankind, or by the history of society and of the world. *Our great internal teacher of religion is, as I have said in an earlier part of this Essay, our Conscience.* [*my italics*] (p. 251)

Newman does not mince words here. He speaks with a boldness I could not have mustered on my own because I am not as sure of myself as he was. That's why I made him my mentor, one who can lead the way for me.

Newman continues driving home his point:

> Conscience is a personal guide, and I use it because I must use myself; I am as little able to think by any mind but my own as to breathe with another's lungs. Conscience is nearer to me than any other means of knowledge. And as it is given to me, so also is it given to others; and being carried about by every individual in his own breast, and requiring nothing besides itself, it is thus adapted for the communication to each separately

> of that knowledge which is most momentous to him individually,—adapted for the use of all classes and conditions of men, for high and low, young and old, men and women, independently of books, of educated reasoning, of physical knowledge, or of philosophy. [my italics] Conscience, too, teaches us, not only that God is, but what He is; it provides for the mind a real image of Him, as a medium of worship; it gives us a rule of right and wrong, as being His rule, and a code of moral duties. Moreover, it is so constituted that, if obeyed, it becomes clearer in its injunctions, and wider in their range, and corrects and completes the accidental feebleness of its initial teachings. Conscience, then, considered as our guide, is fully furnished for its office.

Note that Newman is not speaking just of Catholics. He is speaking of human beings in general. The fact that people are human entails the fact that they have a conscience. Like John Henry in the Legends of the Railroad, Newman is a steel driving man laying down the track along which good people, not just Catholics, should conduct their lives. In his insistence, he is like St. Paul telling the Romans, pagans all, the following:

> For the wrath of God is revealed from heaven against all ungodliness and unrighteousness of men, who hold the truth in unrighteousness; because that which may be known of God is manifest in them; for God hath shewed it unto them. For the invisible things of him from the creation of the world are clearly seen, being understood by the things that are made, even his eternal power and Godhead; so that they are without excuse: because that, when they knew God, they glorified him not as God, neither were thankful; but became vain in their imaginations, and their foolish heart was darkened. Professing themselves to be wise, they became fools, and changed the glory of the uncorruptible God into an image made like to corruptible man, and to birds, and fourfooted beasts, and creeping things. Wherefore God also gave them up to uncleanness through the lusts of

their own hearts, to dishonour their own bodies between themselves: who changed the truth of God into a lie, and worshipped and served the creature more than the Creator, who is blessed for ever. (Romans 2, 18-25)

St. Paul was personally acquainted with the Romans. Unlike later generations who had to reconstruct what the polytheistic Romans were like from documents, he lived with them. He sees that through sins they have erased the reality of the One Creator from their minds and substituted their own idols, a substitution which involves unnatural lust between man and man, woman and woman. There should be no wonder, then, that moderns find passages like these to be highly exclusionary, sexist, hateful, undemocratic, unprogressive, and the rest. Will those who speak like St. Paul end up in jail some day? You better believe it! Their speech will be branded as a hate crime!

Newman goes on to elaborate on the traditional notion of conscience in a way that is like a punch in the mouth.

> *Now Conscience suggests to us many things about that Master, whom by means of it we perceive, but its most prominent teaching, and its cardinal and distinguishing truth, is that he is our Judge.* [my italics] In consequence, the special Attribute under which it brings Him before us, to which it subordinates all other Attributes, is that of justice—retributive justice. We learn from its informations to conceive of the Almighty, primarily, not as a God of Wisdom, of Knowledge, of Power, of Benevolence, but as a God of Judgment and Justice; [my italics] as One, who, not simply for the good of the offender, but as an end good in itself, and as a principle of government, ordains that the offender should suffer for his offence. If it tells us anything at all of the characteristics of the Divine Mind, it certainly tells us this; and, considering that our shortcomings are far more frequent and important than our fulfilment of the duties enjoined upon us, and that of this point we are fully aware ourselves, it follows that the aspect under

which Almighty God is presented to us by Nature, is (to use a figure) of One who is angry with us, and threatens evil. Hence its effect is to burden and sadden the religious mind, and is in contrast with the enjoyment derivable from the exercise of the affections, and from the perception of beauty, whether in the material universe or in the creations of the intellect. This is that fearful antagonism brought out with such soul-piercing reality by Lucretius, when he speaks so dishonourably of what he considers the heavy yoke of religion, and the "æternas pœnas in morte timendum;" [the fear of everlasting punishment at death] and, on the other hand, rejoices in his "Alma Venus," "quæ rerum naturam sola gubernas." [Bountiful Venus, the sole governor of nature.] And we may appeal to him for the fact, while we repudiate his view of it. (p. 251-252)

I find the most startling element in this passage to be the assertion that the most prominent feature of the conscience possessed by us all is that God is our Judge. This is not because God sees Himself this way. In Himself He is loving, benevolent, kind. But his gracious gesture of creating creatures has been met by a rebellion starting with Lucifer and his cohorts and with Adam and Eve as their bodily counterparts. With this rebellion God is justifiably angry. So He threatens punishment not just that we might repent. While God wishes our repentance, that is not His entire motive. There is His justice that must be satisfied. Thus He casts Lucifer and the fallen angels into a hell *that lasts for all eternity*. He does not give them a second chance, which He does give to humans. Even so, if humans die unrepenting of their sins, they too will be punished for all eternity. The justice of God demands that there be retribution. Those who have rebelled against the divine order must suffer the fruits of their rebellion. They must be paid back for their misdeeds. An eternity in hell is the price. Many of us are tempted to overlook this teaching.

Newman then cites Lucretius, a pagan who chooses to see the benevolent side of Nature as the bountiful Venus who governs the world with beauty and kindness, quite opposite to the vengeful way of a supposedly just God seeking retribution. With a few quick strokes, Newman pairs off the opposition between a loving God and a just God, between a man conscious of his dignity as an intelligent and refined human being and a cringing slave trying to placate a vengeful master. The religious mind is burdened by this image of a just God while the supposedly well-adjusted pagan rejoices in all that Bountiful Venus has given him.

Whose side is Newman on? More than most, he was quite sensitive to the appeal of the Greek and Roman authors of the classical age who, unlike their ancestors in a pre-historical age who latched onto a darker form of religion, used their refined reason to depict gods and goddesses dancing about grabbing all the pleasure and beauty their civilized hearts desired. But Newman sides with the primitives, not the enlightened. This judgment about civilized societies is not new to him. In a sermon given in 1834, he proclaims: "I will not shrink from uttering my firm conviction, that it would be a gain to this country, were it vastly more superstitious, more bigoted, more gloomy, more fierce in its religion, than at present it shows itself to be."

I note these points to alert the reader to the fact that when Newman speaks of conscience and natural religion, he does not automatically sympathize with the civilized. While having good manners gives the appearance of being more virtuous, it is often but a cover for deep corruption within. All in all, taking Newman seriously can be quite disturbing.

An Objection

Let me close by going back to the way Newman concludes Chapter Five. Some raise the objection that one need not pay attention to creeds or dogmas because they lead to a cold or merely formal practice of religion. Newman grants that such may be the case in some instances. There is a kind of notional belief which is characteristic of some religious thinkers who see creeds primarily as expressions of the truth and only secondarily as commands to get on their knees. Their belief is correct--but cold. Such belief, however, is not necessarily the result of taking dogmas seriously. It is the result of not taking conscience seriously. Once, however, a person having a merely notional belief begins to pay attention to his conscience, he effects a union between his heart and his head, between holding a truth and living it.

Endure for a While

Newman then gives a key argument showing how propositions or dogmas are essential to religion. A theology may endure for a while without the aid of religion. There is such a thing as credence. But true religion cannot long survive without the aid of a vigorous theology. The emotions of man are ever in want of direction. A father is an object worthy of respect for the simple reason that he is a father. God is an object worthy of worship for the simple reason that he is God. Now it is notional propositions which, in expressing these objects as truths, give ultimate direction to how man's feelings are to be engaged. Just as emotion should follow upon real objects, so religion should follow upon sound creed. On this view of the matter, the young need a clear understanding of their catechism even though much of its teaching may not immediately engage their emotions. Life itself, not some mere pedagogical presentation of a glossy book with pictures, will supply the experience to make the lessons of the catechism real.

Balanced Account of Religion

In showing the relationship between notional and real assent, Newman is providing a Catholic with a balanced account of religion. Just how balanced this account is may be judged from the imbalance of what has happened in the Catholic Church in America for the last fifty years. There has been a great drop in the practice of confession. The teaching that men are sinners in need of redemption has been displaced in the minds of many with the notion that, since God is love, religion should become a joyful affair in which

Christians can celebrate their love for one another and for God. Consequently, the severe and demanding aspects of religion are put aside in favor of celebrations which are not overly concerned with dogmas or creeds--or sin. This shift in attitude is an offense against, not just revealed religion, but against natural religion. If man is not a sinner in need of redemption, why should he accept the authority of the Church as if he were a poor sheep in need of guidance? Why should he not attempt to change the old Church, which impressed an immigrant population with the darker aspects of religion like the existence of Purgatory and Hell, into a new Church with a more positive regard for educated Americans who feel that most people like themselves will go to heaven?

Belief in the Holy Trinity (p. 83)

The second belief which Newman treats is that of the Holy Trinity. Some consider this dogma to be a kind of puzzle that God imposes upon man to show the limitations of reason. Newman begs to differ. It is true that the doctrine of the Holy Trinity is beyond the range of human reason and can be known by man only because God has revealed it through the teachings of the Church. It is also true that the Church has taught this mystery in the formula that God has one nature while being Three Divine Persons. But does that mean this dogma can be apprehended only as an abstraction? Newman answers no.

He notes that the words of Father, Son, and Holy Spirit have come to us through concrete illustrations in the New and the Old Testament. Thus they supply us with images of how these divine persons operate in human affairs. These divinely revealed images, then, allow the feelings of awe, love, and veneration that characterize the practice of religion. Indeed, it is these images which have provided the driving force behind Christianity. Newman could have noted that it was the sign of the cross illuminated in the sky that inspired the then pagan Emperor Constantine to his victory. The sign of the cross, which is made numberless times in the liturgy of the Church and in the lives of Catholics, provides a great example of how the image of the Holy Trinity may permeate the lives of those who have but a shadowy notion of what is meant by the terms "one nature" and "three persons". Further, the sign of the cross, which unites the mystery of Christ's death on the cross with the Holy Trinity in heaven, is distinct to Christianity, marking it off from the religion of the Pagans, Jews, Moslems, and Protestants. Furthermore, the symbol of an empty cross is not the same as a cross with Christ nailed to it. The truth that Christ has saved us from our sins does not save us from the fate of also hanging on a cross like our Master. The reverent making of the Sign of the Cross, then, is testament to how a belief really apprehended can lead to the effort to apprehend it notionally. Why should theologians make the effort to comb the Scriptures for the texts showing the Holy Trinity in action if they have not been imbued with a reverence for this Sign? Here is another example of how the faith of a believer gives the drive to a theologian to use philosophical terms to illuminate a great mystery.

Belief in Dogmatic Theology (p. 95)

The third belief which Newman sets out to explain is belief in dogmatic theology. Because the Church demands that every Catholic give his full assent, not just to the truths which he has learned, but to truths which he knows nothing about, critics object that the Church is imposing a great burden upon the ordinary believer and especially upon the learned. For even the learned do not know of all the pronouncements that the Church has made on complicated theological issues down through the centuries. Thus, the objection goes, all believers are subject to an intellectual tyrant which imposes blind faith upon them.

Newman answers by noting the definition of faith. Faith is believing in what the Church teaches because God, who can neither deceive nor be deceived, revealed it. If one, then, accepts the teachings because God has revealed them, he believes implicitly in all that the Church has pronounced throughout the centuries. God of course has not explicitly revealed each and every one of these doctrinal pronouncements. Rather, He has revealed the main teachings which have then been explained, elaborated, and defended by the Church down through the ages. Thus, a Catholic is no more burdened by the command to believe all the Church teaches than a child is burdened by the advice of his mother to revere the words of Shakespeare. Supernatural faith is essentially an act of trust in the word of Divine Authority even if that word is not comprehended to any great extent. Thus faith enables the believer to accept the inapprehensible because he accepts the authority of the Church. In this case, so called "blind faith" is perfectly rational. It gives substance to a religion on earth that leads to seeing God Himself in the next life. Thus ends Part I entitled "Assent and Apprehension".

Overall View of Part One

We are now in position to take an overall view of Part I entitled "Assent and Apprehension" because we have seen how it ends. The ending shows Catholics that all human beings have the natural capacity to apprehend God as their Judge because we are each endowed with a conscience. If we follow it, we get the increasingly strong hope that God will reveal Himself more fully to us, the result being real apprehension of the Holy Trinity. This real apprehension of a revealed doctrine predisposes us to believe all that the Church teaches simply because God has revealed it. For what God has revealed completes or perfects natural religion exemplified in those who follow their conscience. If we do not follow our conscience we will be predisposed to unbelief in the Judge and consequently to unbelief in the truths of revelation.

To prepare us for understanding the truths of natural and supernatural religion expressed in Chapter Five, Newman has devoted the first four chapters to showing that for better or worse it is real assent that shapes the character of individuals and the culture of society. This is so because real assent has the power to move us because of its power over the imagination. The mover is not notional assent, which resides just in the intellect. Still less is it inference which of it very nature is notional. In laying out these facts of ordinary experience, Newman explodes the modern myth that scientific inference shapes the character of individuals and the culture of society. No! It is real assent, real belief, that runs the world either for better or for worse. Once educated Catholics realize the truth about this basic fact, they will have removed a great obstacle to their imagination. Their imagination will be freed to appreciate the power in the image of a flock of sheep constituting the Church.

Chapter Ten

Assent Considered as Unconditional (Chapter Six of the *Essay*)

As The Table of Contents shows, Newman now proceeds to Part II of the *Essay*. Similar to how he handled Part I, he will devote four chapters to ordinary matters and a fifth to religious matters. But this time the topic will be assent in relation to inference. Newman begins:

> I have now said as much as need be said about the relation of Assent to Apprehension; [Part I] and shall turn to the consideration of the relation existing between Assent and Inference. [Part II] (p. 157)

Up to now he has not bothered refuting directly the attack of modern philosophers that in concrete matters giving unconditional assent is always illegitimate. He has simply ignored them, holding that since neither he nor the common folk had any difficulty in assenting to such propositions as Great Britain being an island, he could assume that unconditional assent to the truth of ordinary matters was legitimate if given in the right circumstances. Consequently, he went about his business of showing that assent can be given legitimately to the truth either of a notion or of a thing. Thus, he removed the illusion generated by modern culture that certitude was illegitimate even in ordinary matters, an illusion possessing the imagination of Catholics in higher education especially. He thereby laid the groundwork in ordinary matters for showing that in religious matters real assent or belief in the dictates of a sound conscience constitutes the heart of natural and revealed religion. In part II, however, he will double back to show exactly why modern philosophers are wrong in holding that the probable nature of inference entails conditional assent. Newman now proceeds directly to refute in detail the contention of modern philosophers that assent to the truth of any concrete matter is illegitimate.

John Locke (1632-1704)

In the following, I will summarize the pages in which Newman, quoting liberally from the writings of Locke, dissects the great man's position, taking the regretful tone of one English gentleman having to point out to another a serious flaw in his argument.

At first, Locke seems to agree with Newman, saying that there are times when men accept conclusions that, though they cannot be demonstrated, accept them as if they have been demonstrated. In other words, assent is legitimate in certain cases even when it is preceded by reasoning that results only in probabilities. But, in another section, where Locke has religious matters in mind, he argues that anyone who gives assent to the results of an inference is guilty of leaping beyond the evidence. In the language of his day, Locke accuses such men of being religious "enthusiasts". On this view, assent is an illegitimate act, an example of the desire to believe overcoming the requirements of reason. It is the act that explains the fanaticism of believers who try to base their lives on rigid certitudes rather than upon reasonable probabilities. Locke will scorn the untutored masses, who hold their religious beliefs as if they were definite truths. Locke accuses them of indulging their feelings rather than using their heads. But critical thinkers like himself will know for a certainty that religious assents given unconditionally must be illegitimate. Instead, there should be only degrees of assent ranging from the probable to the more probable. It's degrees of assent that Locke is opting for, not unconditional assent. Thus is the conclusion of the religious believer who has had the opportunity for higher education.

Newman's Refutation

Newman refutes Locke's position by noting its inconsistency. On the one hand, Locke seems to agree that unconditional assent can follow legitimately from probable inference. On the other hand, he holds that in religious matters unconditional assent is always illegitimate. Newman does not go into religious matters but gives numerous examples showing that there are many cases in ordinary matters where people give their unconditional assent following upon probable inference. There is the belief that there are such places as London, Paris, and Madrid. Men who have no direct experience of these cities nevertheless hold to their existence as absolute truths, not as probabilities or even as high probabilities. Another common belief is that we live upon a globe with vast tracts of land and water. Ordinarily, we do not see these matters as beliefs but rather as plain facts. Since, however, many of us have not flown above or sailed around the world, we have accepted these propositions as true because of the testimony of those who have done so. We believe them, despite the fact that eyewitnesses can be mistaken or even lie. We judge that they have not lied or been mistaken in these cases. But this is an assent of belief, not a result of strict demonstration or of being an eyewitness. Though our reasoning about these concrete matters is still only probable, our assent to them is unconditional.

Other Examples

Here are other examples Newman gives:

> We laugh to scorn the idea that we had no parents though we have no memory of our birth; that we shall never depart this life, though we can have no experience of the future; that we are able to live without food though

we have never tried; that a world of men did not live before our time or that that world has had no history; that there have been no rise or fall of states, no great men, no wars, no revolutions, no art, no science, no literature, no religion. (p. 149)

We cannot demonstrate any of these propositions in the way we can demonstrate those in mathematics or metaphysics. Yet, we firmly believe in them as if they have been demonstrated. The above is an example of how Newman explodes a theory by presenting the facts.

Assent may be given with or without emotion. Notional assents are made coolly. Real assents are made with feeling. The fact that there are degrees of emotional intensity does not mean that there are degrees of assent. Assents are either true or false. There are no degrees in between.

Supernatural Assent

The next point that Newman brings up differentiates between assent to a natural truth and assent to a supernatural one:

> Nor, lastly, does this doctrine of the intrinsic integrity and indivisibility (if I may so speak) of assent interfere with the teaching of Catholic theology as to the pre-eminence of strength in divine faith, which has a supernatural origin, when compared with all belief which is merely human and natural. *For first, that pre-eminence consists, not in its differing from human faith, merely in degree of assent, but in its being superior in nature and kind, so that the one does not admit of a comparison with the other;* [my italics] and next, its intrinsic superiority is not a matter of experience, *but is above experience.* [my italics] Assent is ever assent; but in the assent which follows on a divine announcement, and is vivified by a divine grace, there is, from the nature of the case, a transcendent adhesion of mind, intellectual and moral, and a special self-protection, beyond the

operation of those ordinary laws of thought, which alone have a place in my discussion. (p. 123)

The assent given to the revealed doctrines of the Church is supernatural. While there is a similarity between it and the assent given to the truth of strictly human matters, it is essentially different. It is not based on experience. It is based on obedience to what God teaches through the Catholic Church. This can be seen from the fact than when we were children, we accepted the proposition in the catechism that the Holy Trinity had entered our souls in the rite of baptism. We believed because the Church taught it. The same goes for converts. They believe, sometimes with emotion, sometimes without. Whether they feel it or not, they take on the obligations of thinking, speaking and acting on a supernatural level, avoiding any thought, word, or deed that would detract from their faith. If they happen to sin, they go to confession in order to be forgiven. Here, assent is an act of the will prompted by grace. At this point in the *Essay*, Newman is not treating of supernatural faith, the field of the theologian. Rather, he is dealing with belief as seen by a philosopher using the data drawn from ordinary experience.

2) Complex Assent

Newman proceeds to make a very important distinction. He has already divided assent into notional and real. He will now divide assent into simple and complex. He calls a simple assent a belief in propositions like Great Britain being an island. We believe it because we have been taught it. Since we have not run into any serious objections to this proposition, we hold it just as we hold many other propositions. We hold them as true because everybody does. We see no obvious reason to doubt it. But a truth cannot be determined just on the basis of what everybody says. There are also false beliefs that are picked up from society. At this point, we have no certitude about them. We just take for granted that they are true. It can happen, however, that when we see all kinds of cherished beliefs biting the dust, we start to wonder if we can have certitude about the truth of any belief. So, as a kind of mental experiment, we select the proposition that Great Britain is an island. Without doubting it in the least, we line up in our minds all the objections than can be made and then see that each is highly improbable. After this type of review, we can finally announce without any hesitation that Great Britain is definitely, absolutely, and certainly an island. Less dramatically, we say: "That Great Britain is an island is true" or "I am certain that Great Britain is an island." The mental operation is called complex assent and the result is certitude about the truth of a fact. This progression from simple to complex assent is natural. We want to be certain of the truth our beliefs. The way we attain that certainty is by reflecting upon our initial beliefs and discovering by the use of inference those that hold. We wish to be certain of the beliefs we have acquired from our parents and teachers.

The process can go the other way. We had the belief that Santa Claus brought the presents we found around the Christmas tree. In the course of time, we reflected and saw that Santa Claus had definitely not brought the presents. Our parents did. Reflection has led us to do away with our original belief. When we examine our ordinary experience of life, we discover that we have many more certitudes than we might think we have. After reflecting on our beliefs that Great Britain is an island, that we will die, that Moscow is the capital of Russia, that the earth is a globe, or that oceans constitute the major portions of the earth's surface, we become aware that we have certitude about these truths.

A Closer Look

Newman leads us to a closer look at the distinction between simple and complex assent in order to solve this objection of skeptics; namely, that we believers are necessarily dishonest when we propose to give reasons for our belief. How can believers, the objection goes, be objective in presenting their case when they are already committed to their beliefs? Should we not start by being perfectly open-minded, perfectly neutral at the start?

Students today run into the same objection although it is not expressed in so many words. The objection is more like an atmosphere, something whose truth is taken for granted. But if students with a religious upbringing take in this atmosphere, they will be taking in a microbe that will destroy their faith. Students without a religious background will not have a religious faith to lose. But they will be in danger of losing their humanity. For in today's atmosphere even the notion that marriage is between a man and a woman, that a baby in the womb is a human being, that a boy is a boy and a girl is a girl, or that sodomy is a disgraceful act are being contested. The question arises: What is it to be a human being? That brings up the question: Who decides that matter? The typical answer is that the courts and the legislators decide it. What evidence do they use to make their decision? It is supplied by the modern sciences. But here there is dispute among the experts. In the final analysis, these matters are decided in the voting booth. Those who win the election make the laws. Since the elections take place periodically, the laws are apt to change periodically. Such is the result of taking a neutral stance towards the beliefs in which we have been raised. They will disappear into thin air.

Newman's Answer

To answer the charge that believers are not intellectually honest when they seek for reasons justifying their faith, Newman makes a distinction between an investigation and an inquiry. Ordinarily, the terms mean pretty much the same thing. But Newman gives them a special meaning in order to make his point. For example, we launched an investigation when, after stating our belief that Great Britain is an island, we began to consider some of the possible objections to holding that belief.

The fact that we launched this investigation by no means implied that we doubted the truth of this particular fact. We did not suspend our assent in order to meet some standard of becoming detached or objective about the matter to be investigated. Nevertheless, we did face the difficulties we imagined might be urged against this belief and saw that each of them was unlikely. We then reaffirmed our original simple assent, arriving at a complex assent that now gave us absolute certitude about the belief in question. This is an advance because we now have an explicit intellectual foundation for our original belief. It was not absolutely necessary for us to make this advance. Whether we explicitly looked to justify our belief or not, we would still believe that Britain is an island. Nevertheless, we have followed the natural drive of man to support his simple beliefs by further and more conscious assents. The fact, then, that we launched an investigation into difficulties about our original belief does not brand us as being intellectually dishonest. It shows us to be intellectually alive.

Investigation

Now, common sense recognizes this distinction between an investigation and an inquiry. Surely, it must be legitimate for school authorities to teach that Britain is an island and to expect students to accept it. It would be ridiculous for a modern philosopher to demand that the students be so open-minded that they must suspend or cast doubt upon their original belief so that they could conduct a more honest investigation. In this case, the notion of investigating intellectual difficulties as a way to deepen belief is a common place in the education of the young.

Implications for a Catholic

Why, then, is it illegitimate for religious authorities to require that their students hold to their beliefs while they are investigating them? If the authorities really believe that they possess the truth revealed by God and known by nature, should they and the students not hold to it with even more certitude than Englishmen have about Britain being an island? For the Church, then, it is plain common sense to wall off the notion of perfect open-mindedness from the students while at the same time urging them to face intellectual difficulties with honesty.

Assent Considered as Unconditional

This distinction between an investigation and an inquiry underlies the general procedure of Aristotle and Newman in a practical approach to morality or belief. The investigation of intellectual difficulties requires the student to remain committed to virtue while he seeks to explain it. If he begins to doubt, he falls outside the scope of the investigation and then must launch an inquiry to resolve his doubts. These are two very different uses of inferential reason.

Loss of Faith

Yet, it does happen that a youth may begin an investigation into his beliefs and then lose them in the process. This is not possible in the case of beliefs like Great Britain being an island. For someone to lose his certainty here would mean, not that he lost his certitude, but that he lost his mind. But, it is quite possible in the case of religious beliefs in which the investigator is not grounded by religious practice. The student may have had only the notional belief of profession or credence, having believed because he went along with his family. He may have never made a real assent as a child to religious belief because the adults around him were only conventionally religious. Or, he may have tampered with his conscience, committing sins of impurity, thus giving himself a motive for casting doubt on the beliefs of his youth. He may begin to doubt that sins of impurity are really mortal sins. Or, he may never have been taught that such acts were grievous sins. Nevertheless, these acts may still affect him so deeply that, when he becomes aware of the teaching that such acts are mortal sins, he may reject that teaching as being outrageously Puritanical. Whatever the explanation, it is a fact that students sometimes lose their belief in the process of investigating it.

Suspension of Belief

Some students may not go so far as to reject their former beliefs but rather suspend their assent without taking on a new one. They may not be sure that the Church is right; at the same time, they may not be sure that she is wrong. But this, too, is a loss of faith. Or, perhaps it is a sign that they never had the faith. At any rate, one cannot suspend his assent while at the same time holding it. At this point, we can say that if the student is to regain his faith, he is obliged to resolve this doubt. Here we are in the presence, not of an investigation into difficulties, but of an inquiry to resolve a doubt about the original belief.

Practical Investigation

The difference between an investigation and an inquiry gives us more insight into the kind of practical investigation that Newman undertakes. He assumes that the investigators are already good and experienced men. He also assumes that they should give their beliefs a solid intellectual footing. Hence, they do not launch their investigation for the purpose of throwing doubt upon basic beliefs. Neither are they creating arguments to change the mind of skeptics or doubters. Rather, they are proceeding upon the assumption that the students must preserve their commitment to virtue while they investigate its nature. Consequently, many readers today, not understanding this ancient distinction between an investigation and an inquiry, accuse Aristotle and Newman of always begging the question, of always assuming the truth of a matter that they are supposed to prove. These accusations would be correct if Aristotle and Newman were addressing their works to skeptics and doubters. But the realists are not doing this. They are conducting a practical investigation into beliefs already held, not a theoretical inquiry to resolve the doubts of those who never held such beliefs in the first place.

A Gap

Realists recognize that there must always be some kind of gap between inference and assent in concrete matters. The assent cannot be compelled, as in strict demonstration. Hence, one must either give it or withhold it, not in an arbitrary fashion, but according to what one sees as reasonable. Is it reasonable to withhold assent from the proposition that the external world exists because of some theoretical doubts about it? Here we are not even talking about belief but knowledge in the strict sense. Is it reasonable to withhold assent from propositions like the insularity of Great Britain or the reality of London on the basis that witnesses can either lie or be mistaken? Realists answer no, holding that such restraint in withholding assent to factual truths is an abuse of reason.

The Step of the Argument

So far, Newman has shown that giving complex assent to simple assents like belief in the insularity of Great Britain gives us certitude about the truth of such beliefs. The question naturally arises about the nature of certitude. Newman takes this matter up in Chapter Seven.

Chapter Eleven

Certitude (Chapter Seven of the *Essay*)

The atmosphere of an apocalyptic age eats away at our sense of certitude about the truth of concrete matters. Uncertainty reigns even if we hold that assent to the truth of a concrete matter is legitimate. Such assents may be wrongly given. For instance, there was once the belief (the simple assent) that the actual sun rose in the east and set in the west or that the earth was flat, not a globe. The common people were wrong in their beliefs. They had given their assent illegitimately. Modern philosophers use these facts of history to support their theory of unconditional assent to the truth of any concrete matter being illegitimate. Newman will prove them to be wrong by employing the distinction he has made between simple and complex assent.

The Text

He begins the chapter as follows:

> In proceeding to compare together simple assent and complex, that is, Assent and Certitude, I begin by observing, that popularly no distinction is made between the two; or rather, that in religious teaching that is called Certitude to which I have given the name of Assent. (p. 138)

In practice, the Church holds for no distinction between

belief, assent, and certitude. To believe in her doctrines is at the same time to be certain of them. It is a Catholic's duty to be so. This stand conflicts with the distinction Newman has made between simple and complex assent. He proceeds to explain himself.

Point One

> It certainly follows then, from the distinctions which I have made, that great numbers of men must be considered to pass through life with neither doubt nor, on the other hand, certitude (as I have used the words) on the most important propositions which can occupy their minds, but with only a simple assent, that is, an assent which they barely recognize, or bring home to their consciousness or reflect upon, as being assent. Such an assent is all that religious Protestants commonly have to show, who believe nevertheless with their whole hearts the contents of Holy Scripture. Such too is the state of mind of multitudes of good Catholics, perhaps the majority, who live and die in a simple, full, firm belief in all that the Church teaches, because she teaches it,—in the belief of the irreversible truth of whatever she defines and declares,—but who, as being far removed from Protestant and other dissentients, and having but little intellectual training, have never had the temptation to doubt, and never the opportunity to be certain. (p. 138)

His description of the bond between Catholic belief and certitude fits the description of my parents, relatives, and me as a boy. The teachings of the Church were not a matter of mere credence, which is notional assent to general propositions. No. The belief was real but not particularly self-conscious. I believed that Christ was present in the host, Body and Blood, Soul and Divinity. For me to think or say otherwise was a serious sin. It was only in college that I came more directly into contact with Protestant and secular thought. It was only then did I have the opportunity to be certain in the way Newman describes it. In his view, I had real assent as a child which was the basis for implicit or material certitude. When I went to college, I had the opportunity to attain explicit or conscious certitude by reflecting on my childhood beliefs, the result being complex assent.

Newman proceeds to examine the type of argument that would be proper to one who had given real assent to the authority of the Church:

> As to the argumentative process necessary for such an act, it is valid and sufficient, if it be carried out seriously, and proportionate to their several capacities:—"The Catholic Religion is true, because its objects, as present to my mind, control and influence my conduct as nothing else does;" or "because it has about it an odour of truth and sanctity sui generis, as perceptible to my moral nature as flowers to my sense, such as can only come from heaven;" or "because it has never been to me any thing but peace, joy, consolation, and strength, all through my troubled life." (p. 139)

If someone asked me as an eighth grader why I was a Catholic, I may well have answered it was because the Pope was Christ's Vicar on earth. I was, of course, in no position to defend this claim. I was just answering the question put to me. So, too, with any believer who has not had the training to defend his belief in the face of all the objections that can be made against it. He is giving his own reasons as best he can, which is all that should be expected of him.

Newman continues:

> And if the particular argument used in some instances needs strengthening, then let it be observed, that the keenness of the real apprehension with which the assent is made, though it cannot be the legitimate basis of the assent, may still legitimately act, and strongly act, in confirmation. Such, I say, would be the promptitude and effectiveness of the reasoning, and the facility of the

change from assent to certitude proper, in the case of the multitudes in question, did the occasion for reflection occur; but it does not occur; and accordingly, most genuine and thorough as is the assent, it can only be called virtual, material, or interpretative certitude, if I have above explained certitude rightly. (p. 139)

The keenness or vividness of real assent is in itself not enough to justify certitude about its truth. People give real assent to all kinds of falsehoods passionately felt. But the case of a Catholic, giving real assent is not just an individual's act. While it is personal, it is given as a member of the Catholic Church, a society that insists her believers be certain of their beliefs. This requirement to give real assent leads believers to reflections that do attain explicit certitude unless they have the occasion to do so. But they, like my parents and relatives, did not have the occasion. I had the occasion when I went to college.

A Recollection

I remember the day as a freshman when this thought struck me while I was browsing in the library. "Here I am," I said to myself, "certain in my faith that the Church is absolutely right and the modern philosophers wrong in rejecting her. Now, I know for sure that this certainty did not come from reading a lot of books and weighing arguments as a kid. And yet I have this certainty. Am I not in a religious order now dedicated by vows to the Blessed Mother? Could I have made a mistake?" With that thought, a certain thrill of excitement ran through me. I had visions of being free as a bird out from under all the obligations I had assumed as a religious. I could be like other young men in college going about their business without being much concerned with religious obligations. But, I immediately put that thought behind me, thus heeding the words of my novice master that days come in the life of a religious when he is tempted to get free. The grass looks greener on the other side of the fence. At any rate, the bell rang and off I went to evening prayer. I went about my business for the next week or so without thinking any more about my experience in the library.

But the experience must have been working away without my being aware of it. A few weeks later, I found myself constructing this scenario in my imagination. I pictured myself about to say a "Hail Mary". Before I started, however, I would mention to Our Lady that I would have to suspend my belief in her for a while because I was reading famous authors who did not think she was really the Mother of God or Queen of the world. I would hasten to add that I would not be denying her really. God forbid! But I would not be affirming her, either. I would be taking the neutral approach of a scholar. As soon as I pictured the situation that way, I felt ashamed that I could even think of having such a damnable thought. The sheer ingratitude and stupidity of it! Was I to forget the many times I prayed to her and was answered? I vowed that if I ever seriously considered taking that approach, she would be quite justified in sending a lightning bolt or two my way, not to kill me of course, but to singe my hair and put a little sense into my head.

It was only years later that I recalled these experiences, probably because I was reading Newman. I finally drew the conclusion that reasoning includes a lot more that the formal reasoning of philosophers, theologians, or scientists. A great deal of it goes on in us, both the learned and the unlearned, without our being aware of it. It is particularly the real assents children give to the trustworthiness of their parents that gives them their basic direction in life, a direction they often take without full realization of where they are going.

Concerning Secular Subjects

He continues to illustrate his first point, namely that the distinction between simple and complex assent holds for secular matters. The fact that he is dealing with secular matters gives us a chance to observe ourselves simply as human beings like everyone else. This insight enables us to refute the charge that only Catholics hold for certitude. Not so. Any human being who considers the facts of secular knowledge holds for certitude about their truth. He says:

> Of course these remarks hold good in secular subjects as well as religious:—I believe, for instance, that I am living in an island, that Julius Cæsar once invaded it, that it has been conquered by successive races, that it has had great political and social changes, and that at this time it has colonies, establishments, and imperial dominion all over the earth. All this I am accustomed to take for granted without a thought; but, were the need to arise, I should not find much difficulty in drawing out from my own mental resources reasons sufficient to justify me in these beliefs. (p. 139)

Certitude is a way of life for human beings, not just Catholics. Initially we believe all kinds of things--truths, half-truths, and errors. With the experience of life, we reflect on them, reaffirming some (Great Britain is an island), and rejecting others (Santa Claus brought the gifts). Are we not able to take these beliefs and then from our own mental resources turn them into certitudes? Are we not able to attain absolute certitude about the island status of Great Britain? There is good reason, then, to take our personal experience seriously.

POINT 2

Newman proceeds to his second point. He takes us to school again, repeating definitions he laid out in the beginning and then developing them:

> Next, I observe, that, of the two modes of apprehending propositions, notional and real, assent, as I have already said, has closer relations with real than with notional. Now a simple assent need not be notional; but the reflex or confirmatory assent of certitude always is given to a notional proposition, viz., to the truth, necessity, duty, &c., of our assent to the simple assent and to its proposition. [my italics] Its predicate is a general term, and cannot stand for a fact, whereas the original

proposition, included in it, may, and often does, express a fact. Thus, "The cholera is in the midst of us" is a real proposition; but "That 'the cholera is in the midst of us' is beyond all doubt" is a notional. Now assent to a real proposition is assent to an imagination, and an imagination, as supplying objects to our emotional and moral nature, is adapted to be a principle of action: accordingly, the simple assent to "The cholera is among us," is more emphatic and operative, than the confirmatory assent, "It is beyond reasonable doubt that 'the cholera is among us.'" The confirmation gives momentum to the complex act of the mind, but the simple assent gives it its edge. (p. 140)

Consider the difference between simple assent to the proposition "There is an alligator in my backyard" and the reflex assent to the proposition "That there is an alligator in my backyard is a certainty." Both propositions mean essentially the same thing, but there is more power to move us in the first case than in the second. In the first case, there is an appeal to the imagination, the faculty that directly influences our actions. In the second case, there is an appeal to our intellects, the faculty dealing directly with truths as truths. While we have a firmer grip on a truth intellectually, we may have weakened the springs that impel us to action. Newman develops this point about the role of the intellect.

> If . . .we would see what the force of simple assent can be, viewed apart from its reflex confirmation, we have but to look at the generous and uncalculating energy of faith as exemplified in the primitive Martyrs, in the youths who defied the pagan tyrant, or the maidens who were silent under his tortures. *It is assent, pure and simple, which is the motive cause of great achievements; it is a confidence, growing out of instincts rather than arguments, stayed upon a vivid apprehension, and animated by a transcendent logic, more concentrated in will and in deed for the very reason that it has not been subjected to any intellectual development.* [my italics] It must be borne in mind, that, in thus speaking, I am

contrasting with each other the simple and the reflex assent, which together make up the complex act of certitude. In its complete exhibition keenness in believing is united with repose and persistence. (p. 141)

Lest we be left under the impression that the complex assent of the learned is superior to the real assent of the ordinary folk as far as action is concerned, Newman cites the example of the early martyrs. One can die for the faith without having thought out all the reasons why one should believe in it. Believers do not have to be philosophers or theologians in order to witness to the truth, not just with their minds, but with their lives as well. It is for this reason that the Church has made St. Therese of Lisieux a Doctor of the Church. Although she died at the age of twenty-four as an unknown whose knowledge of the catechism was elementary, she was as solid as a rock.

Point Three

Newman proceeds to point three:

> We must take the constitution of the human mind as we find it, and not as we may judge it ought to be;—thus I am led on to another remark, which is at first sight disadvantageous to Certitude. Introspection of our intellectual operations is not the best of means for preserving us from intellectual hesitations. To meddle with the springs of thought and action is really to weaken them; and, as to that argumentation which is the preliminary to Certitude, it may indeed be unavoidable, but, as in the case of other serviceable allies, it is not so easy to discard it, after it has done its work, as it was in the first instance to obtain its assistance. *Questioning, when encouraged on any subject-matter, readily becomes a habit, and leads the mind to substitute exercises of inference for assent, whether simple or complex.* [my italics] Reasons for assenting suggest reasons for not assenting, and what were realities to our imagination, while our assent was simple, may become little more

Certitude

> than notions, when we have attained to certitude. Objections and difficulties tell upon the mind; it may lose its elasticity, and be unable to throw them off. (p. 142)

Reading this chapter serves as a good example of how reflecting on our certitudes can lead to intellectual difficulties. After analyzing our experience, we may begin to wonder if we are certain of anything. After reading an epistemological argument, I have found myself staring at a tree for five solid minutes and wondering if it is really there! Introspection can lead to confusion. Nevertheless, it is the duty of the educated to endure this pain. The goal of philosophical reflection is to understand things better, not to make them disappear in a host of distinctions.

He lists a few of the questions where common sense has to step in and say "Enough!" There are questions

> which call for the exercise of good sense and for strength of will to put them down with a high hand, as irrational or preposterous. Whence comes evil? why are we created without our consent? how can the Supreme Being have no beginning? how can He need skill, if He is omnipotent? if He is omnipotent, why does He permit suffering? If He permits suffering, how is He all-loving? if He is all-loving, how can He be just? if He is infinite, what has He to do with the finite? how can the temporary be decisive of the eternal?—*these, and a host of like questions, must arise in every thoughtful mind, and, after the best use of reason, must be deliberately put aside, as beyond reason, as (so to speak) no-thoroughfares, which, having no outlet themselves, have no legitimate power to divert us from the King's highway, and to hinder the direct course of religious inquiry from reaching its destination.* [my italics] (p. 142)

The will has a role to play even in the most intellectual of endeavors. Even the saints must use their will to put down the images that disturb their imagination, thus robbing them of the intellectual contentment which their demonstrations should bring. They are well aware that this side of the grave their efforts are only human. The complete answers to their questions will be seen by the whole world on Judgment Day. In seeing God face-to-face in the Beatific Vision, the blessed can finally rest in contentment with themselves. For, it is God Himself who will be telling them that they have done well. They have not allowed their religious investigations to deter them from the King's Highway, the proper destination for their efforts and those of the unlearned.

Point Four

Newman closes with a thought that will lead him to the second major part of his argument; namely, the indefectibility of certitude.

> There is another characteristic of Certitude, in contrast with Assent, which it is important to insist upon, and that is, its persistence. Assents may and do change; certitudes endure. This is why religion demands more than an assent to its truth; it requires a certitude, or at least an assent which is convertible into certitude on demand. Without certitude in religious faith there may be much decency of profession and of observance, but there can be no habit of prayer, no directness of devotion, no intercourse with the unseen, no generosity of self-sacrifice. Certitude then is essential to the Christian; and if he is to persevere to the end, his certitude must include in it a principle of persistence. This it has; as I shall explain in the next Section. (p. 144)

Those who are satisfied with merely probable reasoning about ultimate matters are focused on having certitude about becoming a success in this life. Such concern does not a Christian make! To follow Christ and take up his cross is not done on the probability that Christ arose from the dead. It is done on the certainty that He arose. Philosophers must be ready to reflect on their ordinary certitudes to understand their religious certitudes.

Section Two: Indefectibility of Certitude

Newman has already shown that we are justified in being certain of such propositions as Great Britain being an island. He now goes on to show that such certainties are indefectible; they cannot fail.

> *It is the characteristic of certitude that its object is a truth, a truth as such, a proposition as true. There are right and wrong convictions, and certitude is a right conviction; if it is not right with a consciousness of being right, it is not certitude.* [my italics] Now truth cannot change; what is once truth is always truth; and the human mind is made for truth, and so rests in truth, as it cannot rest in falsehood. When then it once becomes possessed of a truth, what is to dispossess it? but this is to be certain; *therefore once certitude, always certitude.* [my italics] If certitude in any matter be the termination of all doubt or fear about its truth, and an unconditional conscious adherence to it, it carries with it an inward assurance, strong though implicit, that it shall never fail. Indefectibility almost enters into its very idea, enters into it at least so far as this, that its failure, if of frequent occurrence, would prove that certitude was after all and in fact an impossible act, and that what looked like it was a mere extravagance of the intellect. Truth would still be truth, but the knowledge of it would be beyond us and unattainable. It is of great importance then to show, that, as a general rule, certitude does not fail; that failures of what was taken for certitude are the exception; that the intellect, which is made for truth, can attain truth, and, having attained it, can keep it, can recognize it, and preserve the recognition. This is on the whole reasonable; yet are the stipulations, thus obviously necessary for an act or state of certitude, ever fulfilled? (p. 145)

Using the ordinary experience of secular matters for his evidence, Newman has shown that we do have certitude about the truth of many propositions. There is no way we can lose the certitude that Great Britain is an island, Moscow a city in Russia, or King George the Third a monarch if we have given complex assent to it. The idea of anyone losing that certitude would be a sign either that they had lost their minds or did not have certitude in the first place. Imagine someone who has grown up with the belief that Great Britain is an island. He then joins a radical group that pledges itself to the view that the island status of Great Britain is a myth cooked up by politicians wishing to isolate Great Britain from the continent. We should not say he lost his certitude about the island status of Great Britain. He never had it. He only had the belief that Great Britain is an island. Beliefs can fail. Certitudes can't.

Point One (p. 146)

In the following text Newman meets the attack of an English Divine that Catholics are mistaken in holding for the infallibility of the Pope. It is a clever attack made by someone who knew a great deal about religion, unlike the unbelievers today who are woefully ignorant about the subject. Let's see how Newman answers him.

> First, as to fallibility and infallibility. It is very common, doubtless, especially in religious controversy, to confuse infallibility with certitude, and to argue that, since we have not the one, we have not the other, for that no one can claim to be certain on any point, who is not infallible about all; but the two words stand for things quite distinct from each other. *For example, I remember for certain what I did yesterday, but still my memory is not infallible; I am quite clear that two and two make four, but I often make mistakes in long addition sums.* [my italics] I have no doubt whatever that John or Richard is my true friend, but I have before now trusted those who failed me, and I may do so again before I die. *A certitude is directed to this or that particular proposition; it is not a faculty or gift, but a disposition of mind relatively to a definite case which is before me.* [my italics]. Infallibility, on the contrary, is just that which certitude is not;

Certitude

> it is a faculty or gift, and relates, not to some one truth in particular, but to all possible propositions in a given subject-matter. We ought in strict propriety, to speak, not of infallible acts, but of acts of infallibility. (p. 146)

Newman uses the same argument here that he used in refuting Descartes. We do not have certitude in the concrete order because we trust in our faculties or in a general principle. We can have it only as it attaches to some particular proposition. We may have faulty memory or be poor mathematicians. Yet, we can be certain we went to the store yesterday or that 3 plus 6 equals 9. Consequently, the charge that we must be infallible in order to believe in the infallibility of the Catholic Church fails. Here, he is not showing that the infallibility claimed by the Church is true, which is the job of a theologian. He is only showing that the attack against it is false, which is the work of a philosopher. In brief, Newman has established that certitude about the truth of a proposition is dealing with a particular fact or notion. Being certain is not the same as being infallible. Newman's argument is not a proof that the Church is infallible. It is only a proof that this particular argument against it fails.

Point Two (p. 149)

Newman presents a second objection, this time to his view that certitude imparts a certain peace of mind or security because it is indefectible.

> Now how can this security be mine,—without which certitude is not,—if I know, as I know too well, that before now I have thought myself certain, when I was certain after all of an untruth? Is not the very possibility of certitude lost to me for ever by that one mistake? What happened once, may happen again. All my certitudes before and after are henceforth destroyed by the introduction of a reasonable doubt, underlying them all. (p. 149)

It would seem that once one has make a mistake by holding an error as a certainty, one has to give up the possibility of ever being certain. Newman answers:

> It must be recollected that certitude is a deliberate assent given expressly after reasoning. If then my certitude is unfounded, it is the reasoning that is in fault, not my assent to it. It is the law of my mind to seal up the conclusions to which ratiocination has brought me, by that formal assent which I have called a certitude. (p. 149)

It should be recollected that certitude follows after reasoning correctly about a proposition. Certitude follows from complex assent. Complex assent involves inference. Simple assent also follows upon inference. In this case, however, the inferences are informal. Great Britain being an island is accepted because teachers and everybody else says so. In complex assent, the reasoning is more conscious or formal. Is there any possibility that our reasoning has led us astray in this particular case? No. Having considered various objections, we can say with utter confidence that Great Britain is indeed an island.

Newman continues:

> *I could indeed have withheld my assent, but I should have acted against my nature, had I done so when there was what I considered a proof; and I did only what was fitting, what was incumbent on me, upon those existing conditions, in giving it.* [my italics] This is the process by which knowledge accumulates and is stored up both in the individual and in the world. It has sometimes been remarked, when men have boasted of the knowledge of modern times, that no wonder we see more than the ancients, because we are mounted upon their shoulders. The conclusions of one generation are the truths of the next. We are able, it is our duty, deliberately to take things for granted which our forefathers had a duty to doubt about; and unless we summarily put down dispu-

tation on points which have been already proved and ruled, we shall waste our time, and make no advances. (p. 149)

For a man to withhold his assent from the truth of concrete matters because of fear of making a mistake is to violate his nature. Man is a creature of progress because he has taken for granted the truths discovered by his forefathers and then moved ahead to make his own discoveries. If people spent all their effort in reinventing the wheel, they would make no progress. In contrast, we have Descartes who out of fear of making a mistake refused initially to give his assent to the very existence of bodies in the world. That refusal is a violation of reason.

Like a Hunter

Like a hunter who has finally caught an elusive prey, Newman hangs on by pursuing his argument right down to the end. He gives two examples. The first is of a man walking in a moon-lit garden who would swear that there was another man present until he finally discovers he is seeing only an illusion due to an odd combination of lights and shadows in the trees. The second is of a witness in a law court who swears that the accused was the criminal but then has to withdraw his allegation after seeing the real criminal. The fact that people have to revise a previous conviction does not prohibit them from finally being certain. The lesson is that previous mistakes should make us more careful in our reasoning rather than rejecting the notion of assenting legitimately to the truth of concrete matters and, consequently, to the certitude that can come by complex assent. Both simple and complex assent involve reasoning. "Errors in reasoning are lessons and warnings, not to give up reasoning, but to reason with greater caution." (p. 149) Reasoning with great caution means reasoning in the right way in the proper circumstances so that assent is really to a truth.

Point 3 (p. 152)

Newman picks up where he left off, saying:

> If in the criminal case which I have been supposing, the second certitude, felt by a witness, was a legitimate state of mind, so was the first. An act, viewed in itself, is not wrong because it is done wrongly. False certitudes are faults because they are false, not because they are (supposed) certitudes. They are, or may be, the attempts and the failures of an intellect insufficiently trained, or off its guard. Assent is an act of the mind, congenial to its nature; and it, as other acts, may be made both when it ought to be made, and when it ought not. It is a free act, a personal act for which the doer is responsible, and the actual mistakes in making it, be they ever so numerous or serious, have no force whatever to prohibit the act itself. We are accustomed in such cases, to appeal to the maxim, "Usum non tollit abusus;" [The abuse does not prohibit the use] and it is plain that, if what may be called functional disarrangements of the intellect are to be considered fatal to the recognition of the functions themselves, then the mind has no laws whatever and no normal constitution. (p. 152)

Simple assents are agreements to what is taken to be true. They may be true or not. Still it is of their very nature to be in the form of unqualified propositions. Should this form be abused because of faulty reasoning, the remedy is to correct the reasoning, not to abolish the form. If we change the form by denying the legitimacy of real assent to any concrete matter, then we have no laws to go by. The use of reason in this framework will inhibit the growth of knowledge.

Newman continues:

> I just now spoke of the growth of knowledge; there is also a growth in the use of those faculties by which knowledge is acquired. The intellect admits of an education; man is a being of progress; he has to learn

> how to fulfil his end, and to be what facts show that he is intended to be. His mind is in the first instance in disorder, and runs wild; his faculties have their rudimental and inchoate state, and are gradually carried on by practice and experience to their perfection. No instances then whatever of mistaken certitude are sufficient to constitute a proof, that certitude itself is a perversion or extravagance of his nature. (p. 152)

Man comes into the world as a blank tablet. He is a potential knower. Through practice and experience, he becomes an actual knower. How actual he becomes is largely a matter of choice and effort. That's the nature of man.

Newman proceeds to make a comparison between the nature of a clock and the nature of man:

> We do not dispense with clocks, because from time to time they go wrong, and tell untruly. A clock, organically considered, may be perfect, yet it may require regulating. Till that needful work is done, the moment-hand perhaps marks the half-minute, when the minute-hand is at the quarter-past, and the hour hand is just at noon, and the quarter-bell strikes the three-quarters, and the hour-bell strikes four, while the sun-dial precisely tells two o'clock. The sense of certitude may be called the bell of the intellect; and that it strikes when it should not is a proof that the clock is out of order, no proof that the bell will be untrustworthy and useless, when it comes to us adjusted and regulated from the hands of the clock-maker. (p. 152)

The clock-maker has designed the clock's bell to strike four times when the hands turn four o'clock. But the bell might ring when it is only two o'clock. Still, we don't throw out the clock. We regulate it according to the clock-maker's design. Similarly, the purpose of man's reasoning is to attain truth. This he begins to do by simple assent to what he knows without paying much attention. His reasoning is informal. Thus what he takes to be the truth is not always the truth, as more experience of life will show him. Since his goal is to know he has the truth, to have certitude, he reexamines what he has taken in, giving his full stamp of approval only when his deliberate reasoning warrants it. Yet, he still may be mistaken, having arrived at a conviction, not a certitude. To remedy the situation, he has to take a new look at the facts and reason more accurately. If he makes a mistake, the fault is not because he is looking for certitude. That's his nature. The fault is that he has reasoned incorrectly, which is a misuse of his nature. He has to learn how to reason better, not give up his search for certitude.

Not Shy

Newman is not shy about facing difficulties. He moves on to consider another natural faculty of man, conscience. Animals don't have one because they don't have reason. Man has one because he does have reason. He is to live his life according to reason, which means he is to live it according to conscience. That is his nature. Newman argues:

> Our conscience too may be said to strike the hours, and will strike them wrongly, unless it be duly regulated for the performance of its proper function. It is the loud announcement of the principle of right in the details of conduct, as the sense of certitude is the clear witness to what is true. Both certitude and conscience have a place in the normal condition of the mind. *As a human being, I am unable, if I were to try, to live without some kind of conscience;* [my italics] and I am as little able to live without those landmarks of thought which certitude secures for me; still, as the hammer of a clock may tell untruly, so may my conscience and my sense of certitude be attached to mental acts, whether of consent or of assent, which have no claim to be thus sanctioned. Both the moral and the intellectual sanction are liable to be biased by personal inclinations and motives; both require and admit of discipline; and, as it is no disproof of the authority of conscience that false consciences abound, neither does it destroy the importance and the

> uses of certitude, because even educated minds, who are earnest in their inquiries after the truth, in many cases remain under the power of prejudice or delusion. (p. 153)

Newman takes the view that conscience is a natural faculty. Why? Because that distinguishes man from the brutes. Reason has its own structure just as a clock has its. Both function according their nature. They are under law. But also part of our nature is the ability to choose how we will think and live. Thus, we are capable of abusing reason, of disregarding its nature. Now, many people try to eliminate the traditional form of conscience. But by that very fact they follow conscience though in the form they themselves have devised. It is impossible for human beings to live their lives by not conforming to a standard rule, be it only that of doing what they want when they want it. This rule is the standard chosen to live their lives. At any rate, the facts of life should not lead us to scuttle the notions of either certitude or conscience. Rather, they should make us aware of the strenuous efforts we must make to put down our prejudices and illusions no matter how much they may happen to appeal to us. Our nature dictates that we must go by reason because we are rational animals, not brutes. However, rational animals can choose to live like brutes. Brutes can't.

Newman closes with a comparison between the modern age and the past.

> In this day the subject-matter of thought and belief has so increased upon us, that a far higher mental formation is required than necessary in times past, and higher than we have actually reached. The whole world is brought to our doors every morning, and our judgment is required upon social concerns, books, persons, parties, creeds, national acts, political principles and measures. We have to form our opinion, make our profession, take our side on a hundred matters on which we have but little right to speak at all. But we do speak, and must speak, upon them, though neither we nor those who hear us are well

able to determine what is the real position of our intellect relatively to those many questions, one by one, on which we commit ourselves; and then, since many of these questions change their complexion with the passing hour, and many require elaborate consideration, and many are simply beyond us, it is not wonderful, if, at the end of a few years, we have to revise or to repudiate our conclusions; and then we shall be unfairly said to have changed our certitudes, and shall confirm the doctrine, that, except in abstract truth, no judgment rises higher than probability. (p. 154)

During the course of a life that spanned most of the Nineteenth Century, Newman underwent many changes of opinion in religious matters. No one can say that he was a stranger to uncertainty. Indeed, someone has said that a primer of unbelief could be extracted from Newman's works because of the thoroughness with which he treats the arguments of skeptics.

The difficulties he had to face came from the great shift in society from the past into the future. At the very beginning of the Nineteenth Century, Oxford University, Newman's Alma Mater, was still run by the clergy, a practice originating in Medieval times. The university still reflected the social cohesiveness of the past. But by mid-century, Oxford was well on the way to becoming a typical modern university with its demand for more news, more diversity, more debate. It would take far more intellectual development than in the past to deal with the explosion of information and diversity.

Point 4

Having shown 1) that having certitude is not to be infallible; and 2) that certitude depends on reasoning well, Newman harkens back to the comparison he made between the feeling of certitude and the ringing of the bell on the clock tower.

> I have spoken of certitude as being assigned a definite and fixed place among our mental acts; it follows upon

examination and proof, as the bell sounds the hour, when the hands reach it,—so that no act or state of the intellect is certitude, however it may resemble it, which does not observe this appointed law. This proviso greatly diminishes the catalogue of genuine certitudes. Another restriction is this:—the occasions or subject-matters of certitude are under law also. Putting aside the daily exercise of the senses, the principal subjects in secular knowledge, about which we can be certain, are the truths or facts which are its basis. As to this world, we are certain of the elements of knowledge, whether general, scientific, historical, or such as bear on our daily needs and habits, and relate to ourselves, our homes and families, our friends, neighbourhood, country, and civil state. *Beyond these elementary points of knowledge, lies a vast subject-matter of opinion, credence, and belief, viz. the field of public affairs, of social and professional life, of business, of duty, of literature, of taste, nay, of the experimental sciences.* [my italics] (p. 154)

He gives us two signs indicating an act of certitude. 1) Just as the ringing of the bell indicates that the right hour has been struck, so the feeling of satisfaction follows upon becoming certain of a truth. Without this satisfaction there is no certitude. 2) The propositions which allow of certitude are limited to matters with which we intimately acquainted. In dealing with them, we can be absolutely sure we have the truth. But beyond these elementary points of knowledge lies the vast subject-matter of opinion and credence. About such matters, which occupy most of our attention, we only have probability as a guide, not certitude.

Newman continues on this point:

> Hence it is that—the province of certitude being so contracted, and that of opinion so large—it is common to call probability the guide of life. This saying, when properly explained, is true; however, we must not suffer ourselves to carry a true maxim to an extreme; it is far from true, *if we so hold it as to forget that without first*

> *principles there can be no conclusions at all, and that thus probability does in some sense presuppose and require the existence of truths which are certain.* [my italics] (p. 155)

There is the first principle that there are bodies in the world, a principle drawn from the fact that we see, hear, smell, or touch them. As far as inference, not direct perception, is concerned, the existence of any particular tree or animal is only a probability. That bodies exist in the world is an absolute truth.

Newman continues:

> Especially is the maxim untrue, in respect to the other great department of knowledge, the spiritual, if taken to support the doctrine, that the first principles and elements of religion, which are universally received, are mere matter of opinion; though in this day, it is too often taken for granted that religion is one of those subjects on which truth cannot be discovered, and on which one conclusion is pretty much on a level with another. But on the contrary, the initial truths of divine knowledge ought to be viewed as parallel to the initial truths of secular: as the latter are certain, so too are the former. (p. 155)

Consequently, this notion cannot be used to invalidate the claim that religion is based on certitude about the absolute truth of its dogmas or doctrines. Here, he is not proving that the Church is right. He is only showing that the claim of skeptics about probability being the sole guide to thinking and living is wrong. Only in Chapter Ten will Newman directly take up his justification for the truth of the Church.

Newman concludes:

> Such on the whole is the analogy between our knowledge of matters of this world and matters of the world unseen;—indefectible certitude in primary truths, manifold variations of opinion in their application and disposition. (p. 156-157)

Point Five

This is a very long section that forces me merely to sketch the difficulties and Newman's solution to them. He starts:

> I have said that Certitude, whether in human or divine knowledge, is attainable as regards general and cardinal truths; and that in neither department of knowledge, on the whole, is certitude discredited, lost, or reversed: for, in matter of fact, whether in human or divine, those primary truths have ever kept their place from the time when they first took possession of it. However, there is one obvious objection which may be made to this representation, and I proceed to take notice of it. (p. 157)

The claim that Newman is making is based on history; namely, that certitude in regard to human and divine truths has never lost the place it has once gained in an institution. The objection is that history shows that certitude in religious matters is constantly losing its place. In the case of science, however, there has been improvement. Up until five hundred years ago, there were all kinds of contradictory views, a sign there was no certitude. But now there has been development to the point where there is a degree of unanimity among scientists today about what is true. But, as the objection goes, in the field of theology there is still chaos with atheists, deists, agnostics, Protestants, Catholics, Muslims, Pantheists, oriental religionists, and the rest, all contradicting each other. Until some unanimity comes, Newman has no right to speak of certitude in religion. He will have the right to speak so only after he has shown that religion has made the same progress that science has.

Newman's Answer

Newman answers that what unanimity found in the scientific world today is not due to a universal recognition of its truth but rather to a few institutions in which the discoveries and thoughts of great scientists has been preserved. To cite some modern examples: How many people today understand the theory of relativity, thermodynamics, nuclear fission, particles, and the rest? Only experts in a few key institutions. Lesser institutions follow their lead. Consequently, it is not as if scientific knowledge has come like the sun shining on moderns. It has come through the efforts of the few whose authority is the light in which everybody else has been enlightened. The majority of people are believers, not knowers like the experts. Could not the same thing be true in religion where the many rely on the few for the truth of their beliefs? To say this is not to say that such is the case in religion. That claim will have to be established on its own merits. Newman's argument only shows that we as investigators should not rush to a negative judgment when it comes to certitude about the truth of religious propositions; we as Catholics will hold by faith to the certitude that the Church is right. But, as this point as far as our investigation goes the matter is still an open question.

Deeper Difficulty

A deeper difficulty may be drawn from Newman's life. As a child, he was a believer in the Church of England. When he was a youth at age fifteen, he came to the realization that the Creator was the center of his life. With this certitude, however, there was the belief that the Pope was the Antichrist. Around the age of nineteen, he shook off this belief and also the belief in the Bible Alone and joined the High Church party with its respect for Bishop as the leaders of the Church. Up to about his early forties, he led a movement in the Church of England promoting more Catholic views and downgrading more Protestant ones. At the age of forty-five, he left the Church of England altogether and gave his allegiance to the Pope as the Vicar of Christ on earth. After that, he said his history of changing opinions was behind him. He had arrived at the certitude that he finally had the truth, a certitude lasting until he died at the age of eighty-nine.

I will leave it to the reader to see how Newman handled the difficulty of having changed so much. But allow me one suggestion of his. Consider the following:

> Now a religion is not a proposition, but a system; it is a rite, a creed, a philosophy, a rule of duty, all at once; and to accept a religion is neither a simple assent to it nor a complex, neither a conviction nor a prejudice, neither a notional assent nor a real, not a mere act of profession, nor of credence, nor of opinion, nor of speculation, but it is a collection of all these various kinds of assents, at once and together, some of one description, some of another; but, out of all these different assents, how many are of that kind which I have called certitude? Certitudes indeed do not change, but who shall pretend that assents are indefectible? (p. 159)

Understanding the full answer Newman gives to the charge that conversions from one religion to another prove that there is no such thing as certitude depends on understanding the difference between simple assent, complex assent, conviction and certitude. A religion is a whole system of propositions, not just a single one.

Point Six

Newman concludes by taking another shot at philosophical idealists. Descartes refused to give assent to his ordinary experience that there were bodies in the world. So, he embarked on a long chain of deductions after which he was finally willing to give his assent to trusting his sense powers. Instead of assenting to the self-evident truth that his sensing of individual bodies gave him knowledge of them, he looked for an outside intellectual standard to verify the truth of his initial experience of bodies. He tried to construct a metaphysical demonstration. In such a framework, it is natural to ask whether there is some outside intellectual truth that can be used as a standard to verify the particular experience of being certain, for instance, of the proposition that we will die or that Great Britain is an island. Newman answers "no," as the following shows:

One further remark may be made. *Certitude does not admit of an interior, immediate test, sufficient to discriminate it from false certitude.* [my italics] Such a test is rendered impossible from the circumstance that, when we make the mental act expressed by "I know," we sum up the whole series of reflex judgments which might, each in turn, successively exercise a critical function towards those of the series which precede it. But still, if it is the general rule that certitude is indefectible, will not that indefectibility itself become at least in the event a criterion of the genuineness of the certitude? or is there any rival state or habit of the intellect, which claims to be indefectible also? A few words will suffice to answer these questions.

Premising that all rules are but general, especially those which relate to the mind, I observe that indefectibility may at least serve as a negative test of certitude, or sine quâ non condition, so that whoever loses his conviction on a given point is thereby proved not to have been certain of it. Certitude ought to stand all trials, or it is not certitude. Its very office is to cherish and maintain its object, and its very lot and duty is to sustain rude shocks in maintenance of it without being damaged by them. (p. 166-167)

Newman then gives two examples illustrating that we may possess two certitudes to truths which we are unable to reconcile with each other. In the first example, he pictures himself as knowing for sure that a certain man has died. But a few weeks later he sees that same man walking about. What is he to decide? He will hold on to both certitudes even though he cannot reconcile them. He apprehends the truth in each case but does not comprehend the whole situation.

The second example involves the subject of evolution, a hot topic in his day that is even hotter today. Newman imagines that all the various modern sciences have concluded that man has evolved from different ape pairs. Scientists conclude there is no original pair like Adam and Eve from which the whole human race descended. On the other hand, Newman is certain of the teaching of the Church that Adam and Eve are the original parents of the human race. He will not abandon that certainty. At the same time he will not argue with the scientists, who are far more expert about the scientific details than he. He will wait things out. He apprehends the truth of his certainty without comprehending it.

Newman concludes as follows:

> So much on the indefectibility of certitude; as to the question whether any other assent is indefectible besides it, I think prejudice may be such; but it cannot be confused with certitude, for the one is an assent previous to rational grounds, and the other an assent given expressly after careful examination. (p.168)

Experience shows that people may hold onto a prejudice or conviction and refuse to consider the facts against it. They refuse to look for rational grounds and continue to do so until their dying day. As far as they are concerned, their prejudice or conviction is indefectible because they want it to be that way. Although often done, this act is not natural to man whose nature is to be rational. Yet, sheer willfulness plays a large role in human affairs. Newman has shown that there is no outside or objective standard which a person can use to distinguish between a false conviction and a true certitude. The only standard he has is a personal one. Now, persons determine for themselves whether they will live by reason, thus subjecting themselves to the ways things really are, or live by their naked will, thus making themselves the rulers of reality.

While there are no positive standards which can distinguish between false conviction and true certitude, there are negative standards which can used. Newman says:

> It seems then that on the whole there are three conditions of certitude: that it follows on investigation

and proof, that it is accompanied by a specific sense of intellectual satisfaction and repose, and that it is irreversible. If the assent is made without rational grounds, it is a rash judgment, a fancy, or a prejudice; if without the sense of finality, it is scarcely more than an inference; if without permanence, it is a mere conviction. (p. 168)

Conclusion

The account above has been a very long one. The key point I take away from it is this. The certitude I have about the truth of the proposition that Great Britain is an island is indefectible. It cannot fail. I have consciously attained this certitude, not by using any outside intellectual standard, but by considering the facts just of this case. Should any one question my right to this certitude, I do not have to resort to an appeal to some higher principle. The plain fact is enough to ground my certitude. Whatever mistakes I have made in the past, I am sure I am absolutely right about this proposition.

Philosophical idealists like Descartes will not agree. While he granted as a practical matter that the material world exists, he would not grant it as a philosophical matter. Thus, he had to prove that the material world existed. But his proof did not succeed. He arrived at trust in his power of sensing. Having done that, he would still have to demonstrate without any shadow of a doubt the specific fact that Great Britain is an island. It can't be done. For him, then, the island status of Great Britain is a high probability at best. It will always remain so because he cannot find the intellectual standard to justify it. Trust in our faculties is not a legitimate first principle, as Newman showed earlier. The ultimate justification that Great Britain is an island is that it really is an island. To know this all we have to do is use our common sense at the starting point of our philosophy. Common sense requires that we believe the report of eyewitnesses to this particular fact even though we have not witnessed it for ourselves. Embracing this belief does not mean we should accept the word of others about facts absolutely in all times and in all places. Our certitude stems from the fact that in this case Great Britain is indeed an island. Descartes will not allow that. So much the worse for Descartes! Armed with insight, we are then free to investigate the certitude possible about other matters of fact in an effort to dispel the fog generated by the procedures of philosophical idealism.

Note that Newman has not yet discussed the certitude characteristic of the Catholic faith. He has only concentrated on arguments against the faith that have been drawn from inadequate accounts of ordinary human experience.

Last Thought

Permit me a last thought. Newman's axiom that ten thousand difficulties do not constitute a single doubt is quite relevant here. We began this chapter with the unfailing certitude that Great Britain is an island. We then observed Newman as he dealt with intellectual difficulties against the legitimacy of certitude that most people have never heard of before. They would not be familiar with these difficulties because they had not the experience of being immersed in the skeptical tradition of English philosophy beginning with John Locke and heightened by David Hume. Because Newman had been so immersed, he had to deal with them. But in so doing he may well have gone over our heads in dealing with objections we may have never heard of, let alone felt. The solution to this difficulty is to cling to our certitude about such propositions as Great Britain being an island. We can use such certitudes like marines who, clinging to a narrow beachhead established on the enemy's shores, use that foothold to penetrate inland. Being confident that we are at least certain of Great Britain's island status, we can learn to be confident of a lot more that about the truth available to ordinary human experience. Having served our time on the ground, we will then be ready to deal with religious matters.

Step of the Argument

Newman uses the distinction he has made between simple and complex assent to show that we can have indefectible certitude about the truth of many concrete matters of ordinary experience.

Chapter Twelve

Formal, Informal, and Natural Inference (Chapter Eight of the *Essay*)

There can be no complaint that Newman is presenting us with a fuzzy argument. He has taken great care to mark his steps as he constructs them.

Newman begins Chapter Eight as follows:

> Inference is the conditional acceptance of a proposition, Assent is the unconditional; the object of Assent is a truth, the object of Inference is the truth-like or a verisimilitude. [a probability] The problem which I have undertaken is that of ascertaining how it comes to pass that a conditional act leads to an unconditional; and, having now shown that assent really is unconditional, [Chapter Seven] I proceed to show how inferential exercises, as such, always must be conditional. (p. 169)

Newman has shown in Chapter Seven that the simple assent given to concrete propositions like the island status of Great Britain leads to certitude about its truth if one makes the effort to reflect upon this belief by reasoning about it. The result is complex assent. Newman next proceeds to show that all inferential exercises are conditional. Inference, which ranges from the more superficial kind leading to the assents of professing and believing and goes on through the more deliberate kind leading to the assents of opinion, presumption, and speculation is conditioned by its premises. This is obvious. What is not obvious is that the conclusions of demonstrative inference are suitable material for certitude. They are not probabilities, even high ones; they are definite truths. But this stand seems to contradict Newman's statement that demonstrative inference is always conditional. It is. But in the case of demonstration a conditional conclusion is not a probable conclusion. It is a definite truth. Is Newman contradicting himself? But before answering that question let us now go the long way around by investigating reasoning or inferring in general prior to our coming to specifics.

Reasoning or Inferring in General

Newman says:

> We reason, when we hold this by virtue of that; whether we hold it as evident or as approximating or tending to be evident, in either case we so hold it because of holding something else to be evident or tending to be evident. (p. 169)

We reason; animals don't. For, we have ideas, which of course are general. We have the idea of men and the idea of dying. We have the experience of seeing men and concluding they are mortal, i.e. able to die. They died, didn't they? The question now arises as to whether all men—those we have not observed-- are mortal. In other words, is the capability of dying an essential characteristic of all men or is it a characteristic just of the relatively few we have observed? To answer that, we reflect on our previous experience of living bodies like plants and animals. They all have parts because they all have organs. The organs can fall apart, be destroyed in various ways, the result being the death of the organism. Since man is also a living body, we are able to reach the conclusion that all men, not just the ones we have observed, are mortal. We have progressed from antecedent, the premises, to consequent, the conclusion. We have reasoned.

Formal, Informal, and Natural Inference

Newman continues:

> In the next place, our reasoning ordinarily presents itself to our mind as a simple act, not a process or series of acts. We apprehend the antecedents and then apprehend the consequent without explicit recognition of the medium connecting the two, as if by a sort of direct association of the first thought with the second. We proceed by a sort of instinctive perception, from premise to conclusion. (p. 169)

In the example above, we apprehended the antecedent (that men are living bodies), then apprehended the consequent (they are able to die) as a simple act. We did not recognize explicitly any medium or connector between the antecedent and the consequent. Nevertheless, one was implied. This becomes clear when we cast this reasoning into the formal shape of a syllogism.

Living bodies (M) are mortal (P)

Man (S) is a living body. (M)

Therefore, man (S) is mortal. (P)

The syllogism makes explicit the medium (nexus or middle term) which explains why the subject "man" (S) is necessarily connected with the predicate "mortal." (P) Man is mortal because, as the middle term indicates, he is a living body. Such bodies can be destroyed by being crushed, poisoned, cut down, or whatever. Now, angels are living, but since they have no bodies, they cannot be destroyed. They are immortal. Rocks and metals are bodies which can be pulverized or melted down, but we do not say they can die. They are destructible, not mortal. Only living bodies are mortal. Man is one of them. We now have a proposition that is true for all men in all places for all times. There are no exceptions. The proposition is not a high probability. It is an absolute truth.

The example above shows that the formal reasoning

embodied in a syllogism is based on our natural ability to reason. The difference between the two types is that the syllogism makes explicit the terms and steps of the argument.

It is now clear that while all demonstrative inference is conditional because its truth depends on premises, its conclusion is a definite truth because it expresses a property and necessarily inheres in a nature. It is the absolute truth that the nature of man entails the property of being mortal.

A Question

Now, let us ask: Does the conclusion that all men are mortal entitle us to conclude that all men will actually die. The answer is no, no, no! We can only conclude to the high probability that all men will die. This conclusion is truth-like, a verisimilitude. While it is absolutely certain that the nature of man entails the property of being mortal, it is not certain that every individual will actually die. There can be exceptions. It could be, for example, that Elias was taken up to heaven in a fiery chariot and did not die. God is not bound by the fact that Elias is by nature mortal. Nor is God bound by the fact that the nature of Adam and Eve is mortal. He granted them the preternatural privilege of being immortal, a privilege they lost when they sinned. The point is that individuals are not just natures. They have their own histories. As such they are beyond the reach of definitions.

Newman notes:

> But we think we may go on to impose our definition on the whole race, and to every member of it, to the thousand Johns, Richards, and Roberts who are found in it. No; each of them is what he is, in spite of it. Not any one of them is man, as such, or coincides with the auto-anthropos. Another John is not necessarily rational, because "all men are rational," for he may be an idiot;—nor because "man is a being of progress," does the second Richard progress, for he may be a dunce;—nor,

because "man is made for society," must we therefore go on to deny that the second Robert is a gipsy or a bandit, as he is found to be. *There is no such thing as stereotyped humanity; it must ever be a vague, bodiless idea, because the concrete units from which it is formed are independent realities. . . . Since, as a rule, men are rational, progressive, and social, there is a high probability* [my italics] of this rule being true in the case of a particular person; but we must know him to be sure of it. Each thing has its own nature and its own history. (p. 182).

The formal syllogism is most exact and certain when it deals with the properties entailed by natures or essences. But as far as the characteristics of individuals as such are concerned, the conclusions are only probable. Newman already prefigured this conclusion in Chapter One when he stated that his interest in the demonstrative syllogism was only in so far as it touched on concrete matters. In such matters, its conclusions are only probable. Only in the case of conclusions about the properties that flow from natures are the conclusions absolutely true.

Another Limitation

Beside the limitation that the conclusions of strict demonstrations are only probable when it comes to concrete matters, there is a further limitation: namely, that syllogisms depend on first principles, assumptions, or presumptions. Now, first principles are the ultimate antecedents. They do not have to be proven because they are self-evident. Self-evident to whom? That's the question! The answer depends on to whom you are talking. Descartes considers it self-evident that the senses deceive him. Hence, he will not use the existence of things-in-themselves as the starting point of philosophy. Instead, he will only use the existence of things in the mind as images or ideas of things. On the contrary, Newman, along with Aristotle and Aquinas, holds as self-evident that man has sense knowledge of things-in-themselves. Here we have contradictory stands. Who is right? The further use of inference cannot determine who is right because of the difference in the basic characters of the philosophers. Descartes holds that his view is obviously right. Newman and other philosophical realists hold that their view is obviously right. It is clear, then, that the formal syllogism cannot be used to decide the matter because first principles precede the demonstrations that come from them. First principles are first. Philosophers vary in what they take to be first. An unbridgeable gap separates them, a gap which formal inference cannot bridge. This being the case, of what use is formal inference?

The Use of Formal Inference

The use of formal reasoning is that it enables philosophers to understand their own views. Thus, when they meet with each other, they can discover if their differences are just a matter of words or not. If they are just a matter of words, the differences can be clarified so that there really is final agreement. Or they may discover that their disagreement stems from a difference in their first principles. Each party considers them to be self-evident. Here, there is no meeting of minds. They differ with each other right from the start and will continue to differ as they develop their philosophies.

Newman concludes:

> Inference, considered in the sense of verbal argumentation, determines neither our principles, nor our ultimate judgments,—that it is neither the test of truth, nor the adequate basis of assent. (p. 186-187)

Inference does not determine our first principles. Our first principles determine the path of our inferences. Thus, even in determining the nature or essence of things there is a radical difference between realists and idealists. For realists, bodies have real natures or essences. For idealists, essence or natures are only creations of the mind with a doubtful connection to things. Nor does inference determine the conclusions drawn about concrete matters. The conclusion that man is by nature mortal does not entail that all men in the concrete order will actually die. The point? The formal reasoning of the syllogism cannot account for the indefectible certitude we have about such concrete truths as Great Britain's being an island, Moscow's being a city in Russia, or the globe's being covered mostly by water.

The Modern Myth

The modern myth prevails that there is always a higher intellectual position from which we can reconcile differences in lower orders. This is true in practical matters. They allow of compromise. Dialogue is in order. But in the matter of first principles there is no room for compromise. Either there are bodies in the world which constitute the foundations of philosophy, or there aren't. Realists hold that there are bodies because we as bodies are in contact with them by means of sense knowledge. Idealists profess to be uncertain because it is possible to ask whether the body in question is there on its own or whether it is a creation of the brain. Are elephants really gray or are there pink ones, too? Instead of settling the matter by taking a closer look at them, Descartes dumps the whole matter by imagining there might be no elephants at all and indeed no eyes to see them, let alone whether they are gray or pink. Mere dialogue or further reasoning cannot settle that matter. You either start with a real elephants, or you start with your own image or notion of elephants. The trains of reasoning diverge from the start; all the dialoguing or inferring in the world will not put the philosophers back on the same track.

(2) Informal Inference

Newman has already shown in the previous chapter that 1) assent to the truth of concrete propositions like Great Britain being an island is legitimate, and in this chapter that 2) formal inference cannot demonstrate the truth of any concrete matter. Yet, we already know we can know with certitude the truth of concrete propositions. He now proceeds to investigate informal inference for a possible solution to the problem.

> It is plain that formal logical sequence is not in fact the method by which we are enabled to become certain of what is concrete; and it is equally plain, from what has been already suggested, what the real and necessary method is. It is *the cumulation of probabilities*, [my italics] independent of each other, arising out of the nature and circumstances of the particular case which is under review; probabilities too fine to avail separately, too subtle and circuitous to be convertible into syllogisms, too numerous and various for such conversion, even were they convertible. (p. 187)

The real and necessary method for attaining certitude about the truth of concrete matters is informal inference, the accumulation of various stands of probabilities into one bundle, so to speak. It cannot be put down on paper like a formal syllogism can. The first example is our old workhorse, the belief that Great Britain is an island. He shows all the propositions you would have to consider if you were trying to give a formal proof of this proposition. The point is that there is no single syllogism that demonstrates the insularity of Great Britain with the same rigor we can demonstrate that man is mortal. Instead, there are a host of propositions that are probabilities. Even when we bind them all together, we get a very high probability, not an absolute truth. Seeing, however, that all the probabilities point to or converge on the proposition that Great Britain is an island, we give our informal inferences a little bit of a push over the line, assenting with certitude that Great Britain is indeed an island.

That I Shall Die

Another example that Newman uses is the proposition "I shall die." He goes through all the reasons that might be given to put his prediction on the same level as a geometrical or metaphysical proof. He can't do it. All the reasons he gives only approach the future fact but none nail it down.

Completes the Efforts

Newman has used the term "informal inference" to describe the way the living mind of man completes the efforts of formal reasoning by a method that may not easily be marked down in other syllogisms or formal expressions. It is relatively formless; but therein lays its effectiveness. It does not disdain the use of formal reasoning but rather supplements it. But, in supplementing formal reason, it leads us off the clear line of a path marked with the definite signposts of logic into a forest of paths that only the experienced traveler can negotiate.

First Step

Newman's view of converging probabilities is the first step he takes in showing how inference operates in such concrete matters of fact like the insularity of Great Britain, the innocence or guilt of an accused murderer, the fact that Christ founded the Church, the fact of Alexander the Great's conquests, etc. These things of their very nature did not have to happen. But if we determine that they did happen, it was not by the use of formal inference. It was by the use of informal inference that one takes many different strands of probability, sees how they all converge towards the truth of a matter of fact, and judges the fact to be so.

First Principles Again

Understanding the informal method of using converging probabilities makes it easier to understand how the mind attains the truth about concrete matters. But it also brings up the role of first principles. Though his theory of converging probabilities helps us, it is not by itself the complete solution to all the intellectual difficulties about knowledge.

Much of our reasoning happens below our consciousness. In a sermon, Newman once compared the movement of a man moving towards a concrete truth to that of a mountaineer climbing up a steep precipice. In general, he knows what he must do to get to the top and to avoid getting himself killed.

But in particular he must leave it to his instincts, honed from past experience, to find the proper places for his hands and feet as he seeks the cracks in the rock surface that will give him the holds by which he can pull himself up. He arrives at the top but without a precise idea of every movement he has made to get there. Such is a good analogy for the highly personal and mysterious way in which man arrives at knowledge of a concrete truth.

3) Natural Inference

Newman then gives many examples of how people with great experience in their fields reason from antecedent to consequent in a single leap, so to speak. They move from thing to thing, not from idea to idea. Another way to express the matter is to say that they move from an implicit view to an explicit view in a single move. An old farmer looks at the weather in the morning and predicts rain in the evening and is laughed at by city slickers. But he turns out to be right even though he cannot defend himself in argument. He sticks with his long experience of the weather in his local area. Again, a holy woman with little knowledge of formal theology is able to detect heresy in a theological treatise that specialists miss. Her experience of living the faith gives her eyes that specialists with less holiness don't have. Again: Napoleon from atop a hill is able with his spyglass to survey enemy forces of seventy thousand and after a few minutes tell how long it will take them to assemble for an attack. He has the eye of experience which less experienced commanders do not have. Again: A woman looks at a partner whom her husband trusts and is sure there is a crook beneath the fine appearance. The husband laughs at her but to his chagrin finds out that his wife was right when the gentleman later runs off with all the money in the bank account. An old judge tells a young judge to lay down the law firmly but refrains from giving his reasons for doing so. He is apt to be right about the decision but wrong about the reasons.

Newman is not saying that we should trust all those who

insist that they are right. Fanatics, the invincibly prejudiced, nuts and screwballs show the same trust in their own views. Nevertheless, we should not automatically distrust people if they are unable to uphold their views in argument. We have to leave room in our judgment for the exceptions because the wide experience of life shows that mastery of the tools of formal argument is not a guarantee that the expert is right.

It is interesting to note, then, how Newman, a master controversialist expert in the ways of formal argument, insists on a more natural way the truth is attained. It is intensely personal. In maintaining this view, he notes a similar view in Aristotle, his secular master who invented and used the syllogism to great effect. The ancient Greek's concern with the syllogism, however, did not blind him to the fact that sense knowledge acquired by long experience is superior to the use of the syllogism. Quoting Aristotle, Newman says:

> "We are bound to give heed to the undemonstrated sayings and opinions of the experienced and aged, not less than to demonstrations; because, from their having the eye of experience, they behold the principles of things." Instead of trusting logical science, we must trust persons, namely, those who by long acquaintance with their subject have a right to judge. And if we wish ourselves to share in their convictions and the grounds of them, we must follow their history, and learn as they have learned. We must take up their particular subject as they took it up, beginning at the beginning, give ourselves to it, depend on practice and experience more than on reasoning, and thus gain that mental insight into truth, whatever its subject-matter may be, which our masters have gained before us. By following this course, we may make ourselves of their number, and then we rightly lean upon ourselves, directing ourselves by our own moral or intellectual judgment, not by our skill in argumentation. (p. 221)

While the formal reasoning of the syllogism is an aid to

understanding the necessities involved in the nature of bodies, bodies themselves are not just natures. They have a history of interacting with other bodies in unpredictable ways. One age is never exactly the same as another age. Of course, there is a similarity between ages because human nature remains human nature. But this nature is open to either growth or decay depending how people choose to behave. Man is a variable in the way brute animals aren't. If a man is to get the truth about what is happening around him, he relies on those who have preceded him on the road of life. As the child trusts in the words of its mother, the youth trusts in the words of his teachers, so the beginners in a field trust those who have been in the field longer than they. He gets schooled in the facts of life, the human condition.

Newman Exemplified

Newman exemplified these points in his *Essay*. As an old man, he had sensed a change in the culture which was a disease rather than a healthy growth. The modern age will be an apocalypse, not a progress. It will be a radical break from its roots in Western Civilization and in the Catholic Church. So that we will be able to keep our balance amid these changes, he formulates a grammar, a vocabulary that he has found useful on his road to the truth. Without breaking with the long tradition exemplified in such giants as Aristotle or Aquinas, he introduced the terms "assent," "inference," and "apprehension," illustrated them with numerous examples, all in the hope that this knowledge will get us to reflect upon what our basic experience is and thereby enable us to see through the illusions generated by the powers-that-be in the modern age. He seeks to empower us with insight by putting us through a rehabilitation that touches our imagination as well as our intellect. It is real apprehension followed by real assent or belief that makes us tick. He is the kind of elder whose company we seek. He is the one with whom we should stick around in order to get a good grip upon the way we really work, an insight that will tell us in general how human beings work.

Newman concludes as follows:

> This doctrine, stated in substance as above by the great philosopher of antiquity, is more fully expounded in a passage which he elsewhere quotes from Hesiod. "Best of all is he," says that poet, "who is wise by his own wit; next best he who is wise by the wit of others; but whoso is neither able to see, nor willing to hear, he is a good-for-nothing fellow." Judgment then in all concrete matter is the architectonic faculty; and what may be called the Illative Sense, or right judgment in ratiocination, is one branch of it. (p. 221)

Moderns recoil at the thought of being wise because they have believed in the words of others wiser than they. Is not everybody entitled to his or her own opinion and free to express it? Are they not Americans and so equal to each other. Furthermore, why should we accept the existence of an Almighty God who will judge us in the afterlife simply because previous ages held that belief? Why should the belief of unscientific ages be taken seriously by us who have had the good fortune in live in a scientific age? Especially revolting is the belief that there is eternal punishment in hell for those who die unrepentant in their so-called sins? Is it not the real assent or belief in the existence of hell that illustrates the slavish spirit of the past, not just its weak mindedness? Here, we see that the power of unbelief is found, not so much in the intellect, but in the imagination.

Step of the Argument

Newman has shown that the ultimate control of reasoning or assenting resides in the whole man, a combination of the powers of sensation, imagination, and intellection. Man is the creator of the language he uses in his effort to understand the world. He chooses the first principles he considers to be self-evident.

Chapter Thirteen

The Illative Sense (Chapter Nine of the *Essay*)

Newman is closing in on the key notion for which he has been preparing us since the beginning or Part II entitled "Assent and Inference"; namely the illative sense.

Newman begins by reviewing the method of argument he has been using:

> My object in the foregoing pages has been, not to form a theory which may account for those phenomena of the intellect of which they treat, viz. those which characterize inference and assent, *but to ascertain what is the matter of fact as regards them,* [my italics] that is, when it is that assent is given to propositions which are inferred, and under what circumstances. (p. 222)

In sticking to the facts, he has avoided the a priori method of modern philosophers. They argue that since inferences about concrete matters are only probably true, it has to be that assent is given to the truth of a probability, not a definite truth. Now from the very beginning Newman has agreed that inferences in concrete matters are at best only probably true. Indeed, he has spent the whole of Chapter Eight showing that formal, informal, and natural inference reach only probabilities in concrete matters. But instead of jumping to conclusions, he has considered the facts of ordinary experience. They show that we are certain, indefectibly certain, of the truth of such propositions as Great Britain's being an island. In their ordinary moments, modern philosophers will admit this. But when challenged, they profess to hold these beliefs as only probably true. They defend their theory without any regard for the plain facts.

Newman has also avoided the use of the schoolman's method, saying:

> How it comes about that we can be certain is not my business to determine; *for me it is sufficient that certitude is felt.* [my italics] This is what the schoolmen, I believe, call treating a subject in facto esse, in contrast with in fieri. (p. 222)

Newman is not against using the schoolmen's method, which I take to be that of Aristotle and Aquinas. He is only pointing out that he himself is not using it. He has been content to analyze ordinary experience to show when certitude is felt by ordinary folk. In doing so, he has been in accord with the ancients. All agree that there are facts which stand on their own; namely, that man has immediate and certain knowledge that there are bodies in the world. Taking this for granted, Newman goes on to show that we can be certain of the truth of such beliefs as Great Britain's being an island or the majority of the earth's surface being covered by seas and oceans. We discover these facts by reasoning about the trustworthiness of eyewitnesses, reasoning that leads only to probable conclusions. Nevertheless, in certain cases like the ones presented above, we assent with indefectible certitude to their truth. These are the facts. We can then go on to explain them in a metaphysical context if we wish. But the explanation in terms of ultimate causes does not make a fact more a fact. We don't need a metaphysical proof to be certain of the beliefs mentioned above. An examination of our own experience in accepting these beliefs as certainly true is enough for a realist.

The Illative Sense

As we have seen so often, Newman resorts to the use of language to hammer home the way we actually speak and think. To have this knowledge, we have not needed any great knowledge of philosophy. Indeed, if we have had any previous training in it, we most probably have been tainted with some form of philosophical idealism. We would have gotten no help from Descartes, Locke, Hume, or Kant in arriving at certitude about the truth of concrete propositions. Instead, we would have been perplexed by the distinctions these philosophers have made whether they were rationalists, empiricists, phenomenologists, existentialists, or even certain schools of scholastics. In an apocalyptic age, Newman has to get beneath all the words and to affirm us in the way we actually think despite any philosophical training we may have had to the contrary. Philosophy taught and learned in a skeptical age develops more skeptics. But philosophy can be learned right if one follows the approach of Newman and the ancients; namely, to acknowledge the truth of facts before attempting to explain them in metaphysics.

He has gone against the tide, giving numerous examples of how we actually reason. What we are to realize is this: "Every one who reasons, is his own center; and no expedient for attaining a common measure of minds can reverse this truth." (p. 222). "Attaining a common measure" is the key phrase. As we have seen, there is no common measure when it comes to first principles. Realists consider it self-evident that bodies like rocks, plants, animals or men exist in the world. Idealists don't. Right from the beginning there is direct opposition. Realists then go on to develop their philosophy while idealists go on to develop theirs. There is no middle position. There is no higher ground upon which the dispute can be settled. Syllogisms cannot be used for this purpose because they derive their worth from the first principles assumed to be self-evident.

This conclusion prompts Newman to ask the key question:

But then the question follows, is there any criterion of

> the accuracy of an inference, such as may be our warrant that certitude is rightly elicited in favour of the proposition inferred, since our warrant cannot, as I have said, be scientific? *I have already said that the sole and final judgment on the validity of an inference in concrete matter is committed to the personal action of the ratiocinative faculty, the perfection or virtue of which I have called the Illative Sense, a use of the word "sense" parallel to our use of it in "good sense," "common sense," a "sense of beauty," &c.;—and I own I do not see any way to go farther than this in answer to the question.* (Italics mine) (p. 222)

Newman has nothing further to add. When it comes to the first principle of whether or not the existence of natural bodies is self-evident, the stands of realists like Aristotle and idealists Descartes are absolutely, clearly, and definitely opposed. There can be no bridge between them. There is no common ground to settle the dispute. Does that mean there is no way to attain the truth about this critical matter? Of course there is. According to Newman, man's ability to reason must be perfected or completed by the intellectual virtue he calls the illative sense. Its existence, however, is based on the realist's presumption that men are by nature certain of the existence of natural bodies in this world. The possession of the illative sense enables Newman and other realists to explain and defend this stand against idealists who of course oppose it. There are irreconcilable differences.

Then, why do we today have the feeling that prompts us to seek a standard outside of our own center? It is the habit of mind induced by the practice of Descartes to disregard the natural certitude human beings have from the beginning. It is to refuse giving our assent to the existence of bodies in the world because it conflicts with the spirit of the age. Taking this path from what is natural is a decision to be unnatural, to be a master rather than a servant of reality. To avoid this disaster, man needs an addition to what his nature has provided. He needs to make the effort to acquire a habit which perfects his use of reason. That habit is the illative

The Illative Sense

sense. This sense is formed by those living in a community of those with great experience in life and beginners with less experience. The inexperienced imitate the ways of their elders absorbing by osmosis, so to speak, the undemonstrated saying of the elders. The young give the old the benefit of the doubt. This is Newman's final word on the matter after an exhaustive (and exhausting) analysis of ordinary experience. No further proof is needed.

Newman, however, does not leave it at that. Like an English bulldog chewing on a bone, he goes on to give illustration after illustration of the point he has already proven in order to deepen our insight into the facts. He proceeds to do so in 1) The Sanction of the Illative Sense, 2) The Nature of the Illative Sense, and in 3) The Range of the Illative Sense.

1) The Sanction of the Illative Sense

The word "sanction" means authoritative approval or, as the case may be, an authoritative disapproval. The authority which Newman appeals to is that of nature. Repeating myself, I will recall Descartes' starting point. He doubts the validity of sense knowledge. Instead of the natural approach of taking a closer look at mistakes he has made in sensing things, he rules out the legitimacy of sense experience altogether. He doubts not only that there are bodies in the world but even that he is a body. He considers himself to be a pure spirit, an unextended substance or thing, a mind alone. The result is a laborious effort of reasoning to regain his body which he can then use to sense other bodies in the world. He goes against his own experience as a youth when he later decides to become a philosopher.

In Newman's eyes, he has committed the original sin of going against nature's rule. In not accepting what nature does, he does not accept who he is. He is trying to be a detached spirit, not a human being. That is why he seeks a standard of truth outside of himself. Before he started to philosophize, he like everybody else believed in propositions like Great Britain's being an island. But he withheld his assent even to the fact that there are bodies in the world and hence from the fact that Great Britain is an island. He refused to have certitude about this belief because he had other beliefs. Instead of correcting them by taking a closer look at things in the world, he flew off from being an ordinary man to being a purely unattached mind, a kind of pure spirit. He would not submit to the human condition. He wished to be above it. In doing so, he did not have the sanction of nature.

Have That Sanction

Philosophical realists have that sanction, that approval. We believe that Great Britain is an island even though we have never been there. We have accepted the words of eyewitnesses. That's it! We can then at our leisure go on to ask the more general philosophical question of exactly how we as bodies equipped with sense organs are aware of other bodies but, unlike animals, go on to philosophize about them. Aristotle offers us the explanation that we come into the world as blank tablets, as merely potential knowers, not actual knowers. Bodily things inscribe themselves on our sense powers. Our ability to know this tree, that man or those mountains as kinds of trees, men, or mountains is explained by our ability to abstract from particulars their nature or essence. We now have the basis for a full-blown epistemology, a study of the ultimate causes involved in knowing of the existence of other bodies and indeed of the existence of our own body. We now have the possibility of a high altitude dogfight between the adherents of Aristotle and of Descartes. Newman avoids this type of fight in the air by sticking to the facts already known on the ground. He analyzes our language, our way of speaking. He is going to stick to the facts because, unlike the culture of the ancient Greeks and Medieval Christians, moderns have a very weak hold on the facts. It used to be that a baby in the womb was a human being, that a man was a man and a woman was a woman, or that a boy was a boy and a girl was a girl. Moderns are not fit listeners for sound metaphysical arguments. They have no respect for the nature of things.

The Illative Sense

Will they ever get this respect? Perhaps they will if they encounter enough people who have the courage to insist that even in the modern age a baby is still a baby, a man a man, and a woman a woman.

Some Texts

Let us consider some texts from this section on the sanction of the illative sense.

> We are in a world of facts, and we use them; for there is nothing else to use. We do not quarrel with them, but we take them as they are, and avail ourselves of what they can do for us. It would be out of place to demand of fire, water, earth, and air their credentials, so to say, for acting upon us, or ministering to us. We call them elements, and turn them to account, and make the most of them. *We speculate on them at our leisure.* [my italics] But what we are still less able to doubt about or annul, at our leisure or not, is that which is at once their counterpart and their witness, I mean, ourselves. We are conscious of the objects of external nature, and we reflect and act upon them, and this consciousness, reflection, and action we call our rationality. And as we use the (so called) elements without first criticizing what we have no command over, so is it much more unmeaning in us to criticize or find fault with our own nature, which is nothing else than we ourselves, instead of using it according to the use of which it ordinarily admits. Our being, with its faculties, mind and body, is a fact not admitting of question, all things being of necessity referred to it, not it to other things. (p. 223)

Speaking for himself and indeed for anyone who does not wish to commit intellectual suicide by losing himself in the search for a standard outside of himself, he continues:

> My first elementary lesson of duty is that of resignation to the laws of my nature, whatever they are; my first disobedience is to be impatient at what I am, and to

> indulge an ambitious aspiration after what I cannot be, to cherish a distrust of my powers, and to desire to change laws which are identical with myself. (p. 226)

At this point Newman has not yet brought in the notion of God as the author of nature. But he doesn't have to. If we have any instinct for respecting our own nature and that of others, we accept reality as it is and do the best we can with it. We are not talking about holiness here. We are talking about sanity. But finally Newman does bring in the notion of God, saying:

> Of course I do not stop here. As the structure of the universe speaks to us of Him who made it, so the laws of the mind are the expression, not of mere constituted order, but of His will. I should be bound by them even were they not His laws; but since one of their very functions is to tell me of Him, they throw a reflex light upon themselves, and, for resignation to my destiny, I substitute a cheerful concurrence in an overruling Providence. (p. 226)

Here Newman insists that belief in God is part of ordinary human experience. Such experience is the norm or standard for defining a human being. Moderns reject this standard, thereby showing themselves to be abnormal, unnatural freaks. Newman is not speaking just of monotheists. He is also speaking of pagans like Aristotle who, inspired with a reverence for the gods, laid out the formal ways of reasoning that should be used in looking for the causes of nature. The Greek constructed a philosophy, not as a substitute for religion, but as a way of purifying what he already believed. He was fundamentally a religious man showing that the highest science of all consists in the happiness of contemplating the gods through their works. He formulates a natural theology, thus exemplifying the saying that belief leads to understanding.

2) The Nature of the Illative Sense

Newman now begins to be very precise about the meaning of the term "illative sense," which is derived from the Latin word for inferring or for moving from one thing to another.

> It is the mind that reasons, and that controls its own reasonings, not any technical apparatus of words and propositions. This power of judging and concluding, when in its perfection, I call the Illative Sense, and I shall best illustrate it by referring to parallel faculties, which we commonly recognize without difficulty. (p. 227)

He then proceeds to illustrate his notion of the illative sense by analyzing the *Nicomachean Ethics* of Aristotle, which has been part of the history of philosophy since the Fourth Century before Christ. While this work is addressed specifically to the realm of individual and communal ethics or politics, it serves as an example of what Newman means by the illative sense used in getting knowledge of anything in the concrete or natural order. Although this term is Newman's invention, it has its roots in Catholic philosophy. Since St. Thomas Aquinas wrote a line by line commentary on the *Nicomachean Ethics*, we have the testimony of the Common Doctor to the truth of what Aristotle says. The Catholic and the Pagan agree that metaphysics is the highest of the human sciences. The demonstrative syllogism reigns as the way to attaining the truth about the nature of ultimate causes. This way is an objective, impersonal, or universal account showing that the path to man's happiness is the contemplation of the divine. No exceptions are allowed. The speculative science of metaphysics rules. This immutable truth is to be sought for its own sake. What individual philosophers think about it is irrelevant. Period. Now no one can think of either Aristotle or Aquinas as being relativists. Here is the insistence on a truth to be held by all men in all ages and in all places. You can't get any more objective than that.

But when Aquinas, following Aristotle, turns to the task of

men attaining the highest end, he institutes the practical science of ethics. It differs from the speculative science of metaphysics. In metaphysics, the standard of truth is reality itself. Here man's intellect is ruled or measured by its object. In contrast, the standard of truth in ethics is the virtuous and experienced man himself. Let me repeat: the standard of truth in ethics is the virtuous and experienced man himself. It is his judgment that determines what is to be done in the here and now, the concrete order. Newman echoes this distinction between the speculative and practical science in the following text.

> How does the mind fulfil its function of supreme direction and control, in matters of duty, social intercourse, and taste? *In all of these separate actions of the intellect, the individual is supreme, and responsible to himself, nay, under circumstances, may be justified in opposing himself to the judgment of the whole world*; [my italics] though he uses rules to his great advantage, as far as they go, and is in consequence bound to use them. As regards moral duty, the subject is fully considered in the well-known ethical treatises of Aristotle. He calls the faculty which guides the mind in matters of conduct, by the name of *phronesis*, or judgment. This is the directing, controlling, and determining principle in such matters, personal and social. What it is to be virtuous, how we are to gain the just idea and standard of virtue, how we are to approximate in practice to our own standard, what is right and wrong in a particular case, for the answers in fullness and accuracy to these and similar questions, *the philosopher refers us to no code of laws, to no moral treatise, [to no metaphysics] because no science of life, applicable to the case of an individual, has been or can be written. Such is Aristotle's doctrine, and it is undoubtedly true.* [italics mine] (p. 228)

Newman has not turned into a personalist, the kind of relativist due to the influence of modern philosophers. No. He is following the ancient distinction between the person of the metaphysician and that of the moral philosopher. The metaphysician seeks the truth alone. His personal preferences have nothing to do with the outcome. The truth alone measures or rules him. In contrast, the moral philosopher seeks the truth for the sake of action. In the practical science of ethics or politics you don't seek the truth alone. Rather you seek the truth for the sake of action. He is not content just to know what man's highest goal is. Rather he wants to know how to get it. In order to get it, he already has to be both a good man and have long experience in life. He has to have the experience of living in this actual world and to have acquired the virtues of prudence, justice, fortitude, and temperance. Here, the focus is on the agent. For it is only such an agent that can do the right deeds in the right way at the right times in the right places. Now these deeds are necessarily particular, meaning that they exist only in a particular time and place. Consequently, the advice of the moral philosopher expressed in the norms of being prudent, just, courageous, or temperate are too general to be of much practical help. But the young need the guidance of virtuous elders experienced in living. For example, the universal norm of courage tells soldiers to do their duty. But sometimes their duty is to stand and fight to the death. At other times, it is to retreat so that they can fight again another day. What is the right action to take at the moment is known only by those experienced in the heat and confusion of a particular battle. No knowledge of general norms will do the job. There has to be the personal influence of the officers on the men about what is to be done at the moment. In brief, the good and experienced man serves as the standard of what is to be done at the moment.

The same goes for the universal norm of temperance, which states that in matters of food, drink, and sex there should not be too much or too little. The golden mean is to be kept between excess and defect. This norm is too broad to be practical. There has to be on hand the good and experienced person to show how the norm plays out in the variable circumstances of life. No science, even a practical one, can do the job. The virtuous man and woman in their own circumstances have actually followed the golden mean. Without their example, the norms of temperance are mere platitudes which have no feet on the ground. The temperate person makes the norm a reality upon this earth. He or she speaks, not only in words, but more importantly in deeds. Each person forms a nucleus around which others can gather. The result is a community embodying the notion of temperance. That's the way the world works.

There is nothing wishy-washy about their example. They are not examples of situation ethics. Each norm takes for granted that gluttony, drunkenness, adultery, fornication, and sodomy are always wrong. They are intrinsically evil and so can never be right. So, too, for the other virtues. Acts of murder or stealing are always wrong no matter what the circumstance. But there is a lot more to life than avoiding intrinsic evils. There remains the task of doing the right thing in the right way at the right time and in the right place. In this matter, the virtuous person is the sole judge of what should be done. While he or she is aided by the science of ethics, its universal norms are too broad to give direction in the details of life. He or she becomes the rule or measure of what is to be done in the here and now. Each has the eye of experience.

From Upbringing

There arises the question of how and where Aristotle attained the knowledge necessary to construct the practical science of ethics or politics, a construction having great influence on the moral philosophy of St. Thomas Aquinas over fifteen hundred years later. The ancient Greek got it from his upbringing. His parents and elders had given him his love for virtue long before he was able to define it. The games he played, the stories he heard, the songs he sang, and the rules he obeyed shaped his imagination which in turn shaped his character. When he matured, he came under the influence of Plato who, in turn had come under the influence of Socrates, a good man with a giant's intellect. From

Socrates there came Plato from whom came Aristotle, the one whom Aquinas called *The Philosopher* over sixteen centuries later.

Even in the construction of a metaphysics, the good and experienced man holds the tools. The path of discovering the truth about ultimate causes is not a highway all laid out so that anyone can travel it. Only the virtuous and experienced man is equipped to do the travelling. In doing so, he marks his way by constructing demonstrative syllogisms as an invitation to others to check him out. His private way of proceeding becomes public. While no syllogism is precise or subtle enough to reveal his mind fully, it is the best that a human being of body and soul can do. In the final analysis, it is not the syllogism, the tool, that has the truth. It is the mind that constructed it.

It is clear that Newman's illative sense is very much within the tradition of Aristotle and Aquinas. Newman's innovation is to broaden the notion of the virtuous person's being the immediate guide in moral matters to the notion of the experienced person being the guide to anything at all that needs to be done. Living in a community of elders and beginners develops the sense of what is to be done whether it be the construction of a metaphysics, a political community, or an artifact like a ship or a house. Newman calls this sense "the illative sense," a perfection acquires by long practice, not mere study. No one trusts an engineer who just has the theory. To build a new bridge they want one who has already built them. If the bridges have stood up in the past, there is a good chance that the new one will stay up in the future.

3) The Range of the Illative Sense

Newman now begins to show the wide range of the acquirement he calls the illative sense.

> Great as are the services of language in enabling us to extend the compass of our inferences, to test their validity, and to communicate them to others, still the

> mind itself is more versatile and vigorous than any of its works, of which language is one, and it is only under its penetrating and subtle action that the margin disappears, which I have described as intervening between verbal argumentation and conclusions in the concrete. *It determines what science cannot determine, the limit of converging probabilities and the reasons sufficient for a proof.* [my italics] It is the ratiocinative mind itself, and no trick of art, however simple in its form and sure in operation, by which we are able to determine, and thereupon to be certain, that a moving body left to itself will never stop, and that no man can live without eating. (p. 232)

To understand the method of converging probabilities, you have to understand the larger context in which it takes place. It takes place in actual people, not in books or on paper. Now everyone is not able to put together the strands of many different probable arguments to reach a conclusion. Only those who have long experience in the field in question and who have lived with elders in that field do it right. They have the illative sense, which is an acquired perfection built upon the natural ability to reason. It is to reason well. This is above all determined by the ability to start with the first principles appropriate to the subject matter.

Many Examples

Newman proceeds to give many examples of how widely people vary in their selection of first principles. After they select them either consciously or unconsciously, they then create chains of reasoning leading to conclusions. The differences between world-class thinkers is not due to one reasoning better than another. They connect one link with another quite logically. Rather, the difference is to be found in their selection of first principles. If these starting points contradict each other, there is no way to settle the difference by further reasoning. For the reasoning follows upon the first principle selected; it does not create it. As Newman says:

The Illative Sense

> . . . all reasoning being from premisses, and those premisses arising (if it so happen) in their first elements [principles] from personal characteristics, in which men are in fact in essential and irremediable variance one with another, the ratiocinative talent can do no more than point out where the difference between them lies, how far it is immaterial, when it is worthwhile continuing an argument between them, and when not. (p. 233)

We have already considered the radical difference between philosophical idealists and philosophical realists. who take the existence of that world for granted. They are in irremediable opposition to each other. Inference alone cannot bridge the difference. The first principle is either that of a realist or that of an idealist. You might think there is common ground in the fact that both have images and ideas of things in their minds. The idealist suggests to his opponent that they examine these items in the mind to see whether they correspond to bodies in the world. The realist rejects this suggestion, insisting that the existence of bodies in the world is already self-evident. He sees no need for further investigation on this particular point. The idealist insists there is such a need. Each then proceeds down his own path with great consistency. Newman describes his own path:

> I would rather have to maintain that we ought to begin with believing everything that is offered to our acceptance, than that it is our duty to doubt of everything. The former, indeed, seems the true way of learning. In that case, we soon discover and discard what is contradictory to itself; and error having always some portion of truth in it, and the truth having a reality which error has not, we may expect, that when there is an honest purpose and fair talents, we shall somehow make our way forward, the error falling off from the mind, and the truth developing and occupying it. (p. 243)

Going along with the natural way of knowing followed by

most of mankind from the start, Newman trusts that the nature of their experience will over the course of time lead men to the truth about the natural order. There will necessarily be trial and error, a progression from inference starting with profession, credence, opinion and going on to the more deliberate types of presumption and speculation. That's the Human Condition. Errors will be corrected along the way if the travelers stick to the natural path. Otherwise there will be no natural way. There will instead the unnatural way chosen by those who think they have the better way. They will be the generators of an apocalyptic culture.

The Realm of Religious Belief

Newman also treats of the role that character plays in the choice of religious first principles. In the Sixteenth Century, Protestants took as their first principle the tenet that all religious truth is to be found in the Bible, not in the teaching authority of the Catholic Church. So when they challenged Catholics to support their claims, they automatically judged them to be wrong because they could not produce a clear text from the Scriptures proving the truth of such doctrines as Purgatory, the Immaculate Conception, or the Real Presence. It made absolutely no impression on them when Catholics answered that not all religious truths can be found clearly and explicitly stated in the Bible. Here we have an example of a collision between first principles. Catholics insist that there are such a things as verbal traditions that have not been written down. When a Protestant approaches Catholic beliefs, his reasoning is informed by the principle that all religious truth is to be found explicitly stated in the Bible. He has grown up and taken on the presumptions of one type of community. When a Catholic approaches the matter, his reasoning is informed by a different principle. He has grown up in another type of community. Now, there is no question that Newman considers the reasoning of the Protestant to be wrong. He himself traveled the long road from being a Protestant to being a Catholic. But even though he started out as a Protestant, he was the type whose ultimate trust was in God as the Light on the path. Since God's way is not man's way, he was taking a chance. As he followed that way, he dropped the errors that Scripture Alone was sufficient, that the Pope was the Antichrist or that the Anglican Bishops were the descendants of the Apostles. He dropped these beliefs because further reasoning showed them to be errors.

Referring to a piece he wrote as a Protestant, Newman says:

> "It matters not," I said, speaking of the first Protestants, "whether or not they only happened to come right on what, in a logical point of view, are faulty premisses. They had no time for theories of any kind; and to require theories at their hand argues an ignorance of human nature, and of the ways in which truth is struck out in the course of life. Common sense, chance, moral perception, genius, the great discoverers of principles do not reason. They have no arguments, no grounds, they see the truth, but they do not know how they see it; and if at any time they attempt to prove it, it is as much a matter of experiment with them, as if they had to find a road to a distant mountain, which they see with the eye; and they get entangled, embarrassed, and perchance overthrown in the superfluous endeavour. It is the second-rate men, though most useful in their place, who prove, reconcile, finish, and explain. Probably, the popular feeling of the sixteenth century saw the Bible to be the Word of God, so as nothing else is His Word, by the power of a strong sense, by a sort of moral instinct, or by a happy augury." That is, I considered the assumption an act of the Illative Sense;—I should now add, the Illative Sense, acting on mistaken elements of thought. (p. 245)

Even as a Protestant Newman recognized that making Scripture Alone the source of all religious knowledge could not be justified by ratiocination. Nevertheless, he held for a while that the Reformers had been right although their premises were faulty. He made room for the validity of informal reasoning. When he became a Catholic, he concluded that the Reformers were wrong. Why? His illative sense, a perfection of informal reasoning, led him to see that the deposit of faith was to be found in the Catholic Church from the very beginning of Christianity. A knowledge of history led to that conclusion. This knowledge he had picked up from his association with those in the High Church party who studied the history of the Church. He saw that once you take the actual history of the Church down through the centuries, you can't be a Protestant. You cannot put all religious teachings in the confines even of a sacred book. You have to look for a living teaching body explaining the deposit of faith. In doing so, he was proceeding by an illative sense he acquired among Anglican elders who had still held to the old Catholic view that religious knowledge was embodied in a Church, not in a book as sacred as it is. In converting, Newman went beyond his Anglican elders to a new set of elders.

Steps of the Argument

A summary of Chapters Six to Nine is as follows. In Chapter Six Newman refutes the stand of John Locke that inference in concrete matters results in varying degrees of assent ranging from the less probable to the more probable. Newman shows as a matter of fact that there are many concrete and ordinary matters to which people give unconditional assent to a definite truth.

Newman then introduces the distinction between simple and complex assent, simple assent being agreement to the truth of a proposition in an unreflecting way and complex assent being agreement to the truth of a proposition after reflection.

In Chapter Seven, Newman shows that complex assent leads to indefectible certitude about the truth of propositions treating of concrete matters. In Chapter Eight, Newman shows that formal, informal, and natural inference in concrete matters lead only to probable conclusions. Consequently, there remains the task of showing how inference nevertheless can lead to unconditional assent.

The Illative Sense

In Chapter Nine, Newman concludes Part Two by showing the proper relationship between assent and inference in ordinary matters. The key factor in understanding the relationship is that the living intellect of each man does the job, not any apparatus of verbal argumentation or science. At the center of each person lays two choices. There is the choice of taking the existence of the world of bodies for granted and then learning step-by-step in the fellowship of like-minded seekers what nature has to teach them. The experienced acquire the illative sense which gives them command over the right first principle and what follows from it. The less experienced acquire the illative sense by personal contact with the experienced. This is the way of the philosophical realist. Or there is the way of the philosophical idealist; namely, put doubt the existence of bodies in the world and then use a disembodied reason as the way to get the truth. This way is also embodied in kindred fellow seekers. In the modern age, the idealists call the tune.

Chapter Fourteen

Assent and Inference in Religious Matters (Chapter Ten of the *Essay*)

We now come to Chapter Ten, the culmination of the argument that is *An Essay in Aid of a Grammar of Assent*. The first paragraph goes as follows:

> And now I have completed my review of the second subject to which I have given my attention in this *Essay*, the connexion existing between the intellectual acts of Assent and Inference, my first being the connexion of Assent with Apprehension; and as I closed my remarks upon Assent and Apprehension by applying the conclusions at which I had arrived to our belief in the Truths of Religion, so now I ought to speak of its Evidences, before quitting the consideration of the dependence of Assent upon Inference. I shall attempt to do so in this Chapter... (p. 248)

The conclusion he has drawn from the four chapters of Part II is that the individual himself, not any verbal or explicit construct of formal or informal inference, is central to the discovery of the truth in ordinary matters. Essential to this discovery is the attainment of the illative sense, a perfection acquired in a community where the inexperienced imitate the ways of the experienced and so acquire the truths in their various fields. He will now apply his conclusions about the illative sense to the field of religion.

Newman continues:

> I begin with expressing a sentiment, which is habitually in my thoughts, whenever they are turned to the subject of mental or moral science, and which I am as willing to apply here to the Evidences of Religion as it properly applies to Metaphysics or Ethics, viz. *that in these provinces of inquiry egotism is true modesty.* [my italics] In religious inquiry each of us can speak only for himself, and for himself he has a right to speak. His own experiences are enough for himself, but he cannot speak for others: he cannot lay down the law; he can only bring his own experiences to the common stock of psychological facts. He knows what has satisfied and satisfies himself; if it satisfies him, it is likely to satisfy others; if, as he believes and is sure, it is true, it will approve itself to others also, for there is but one truth. And doubtless he does find in fact, that, allowing for the difference of minds and of modes of speech, what convinces him, does convince others also. (p. 248)

Relying upon his illative sense, Newman will speak for himself. He has acquired this sense as a beginner in the Catholic Church when he joined it at the age of forty-five. While he already knew in a formal way more theology than even learned Catholics, he had yet to walk the path as a regular sheep in the flock. Having done so for twenty-five years, he is now ready to speak as an elder. He feels confident in bringing his personal insight to the common stock. The flock will have the ears to hear him. Allowing for incidental differences, he is confident that what has satisfied him will satisfy them. Since, however, his circumstances in life have led him to a wide acquaintance with history, philosophy, and theology, he is particularly suited to address those who are in higher education. Is not their purpose to know in an explicit way the truth about the big picture? Catholics outside the walls of academia have other more implicit ways of knowing the truth. But should not there be elders who can address the educated in their own language? Newman proposes to be such an elder.

Sets to Work

He sets to work constructing his argument. It is a construction after he has experienced all the twists and turns of becoming a Catholic. Out of this personal experience, he will make an orderly argument. The first step he takes is to define the Church which we are seeking to defend. She is the result of a divine revelation. Now, it is possible to think that God could have revealed truths which took hold of mankind without its knowing that He was the origin of them. Instead, God has revealed Himself in a more personal and definite way.

> It is a definite message from God to man distinctly conveyed by His chosen instruments and to be received as such a message; and therefore to be positively acknowledged and embraced, and maintained as true, on the ground of its being divine, not as true on intrinsic grounds, not as probably true, or partially true, but as absolutely certain knowledge, certain in a sense in which nothing else can be certain, because it comes from Him who can neither deceive nor be deceived. (p. 249)

The Church Newman is teaching us to defend is not some vague thing like religion or Christianity in general. She is a definite flock, institution, or society that we have accepted as divine because of her teaching that she is from God who can neither deceive nor be deceived. I learned that as a kid in grade school.

While I also learned the certainty that three times five is fifteen, I had a lot more feeling for the Church that I had for the times table. God was alive; the times table wasn't.

At any rate, part of the revelation I learned as a kid was the Ten Commandments. I was of course unable to distinguish the commandments based on natural religion and those based upon supernatural religion. The commandments were the commandments. Only later did I learn that all the commandments except for the third (Keep holy the Sabbath Day) were based on natural religion. They bound all human beings because they were human beings. Thus, in learning about what was revealed I learned about natural religion, what was inscribed on the human heart without my realizing the distinction. Newman take pains to point this out, saying that

> . . . the exhibition of credentials, that is, of evidence, that it is what it professes to be, is essential to Christianity, as it comes to us; for we are not left at liberty to pick and choose out of its contents according to our judgment, but must receive it all, as we find it, if we accept it at all. It is a religion in addition to the religion of nature; and as nature has an intrinsic claim upon us to be obeyed and used, so what is over and above nature, or supernatural, must also bring with it valid testimonials of its right to demand our homage. (p. 250)

It was the practice of Christ and His Apostles to teach the elements of natural religion as a necessary condition to learning the tenets of supernatural religion. We were to accept all the commandments, having no right to pick and choose among them. The logic behind this approach was as follows. Human beings already had imprinted upon their minds and hearts the dictates of natural religion. Therefore, they had the predisposition to accept supernatural religion when they became aware of it, which they did through Abraham and later through Christ. It is only right, then, that anyone constructing an argument to justify the Church follows the pattern laid down by Christ and His Apostles. You have to start with the more known before you proceed to the less known. You start with nature and proceed to what is above nature. In other words, you start with the dictates of conscience.

(1) The Voice of Conscience

What are those dictates?

> Now conscience suggests to us many things about that Master, whom by means of it we perceive, but its most prominent teaching, and its cardinal and distinguishing truth, is that he is our Judge. In consequence the special Attribute under which it brings Him before us, to which it subordinates all other Attributes, is that of justice-- retributive justice. We learn from its informations to conceive of the Almighty, primarily, not as a God of Wisdom, of Knowledge, of Power, of Benevolence, but as a God of Judgment and Justice; as One, who, not simply for the good of the offender, but as an end good in itself, and as a principle of government, ordains that the offender should suffer for his offense. If it tells us anything at all of the characteristics of the Divine Mind, it certainly tells us this; and, considering our short comings are far more frequent and important than the fulfillment of our duties, and that of this point we are fully aware ourselves, it follows that the aspect under which Almighty God is presented to us by Nature, is (to use a figure) of One who is angry with us and threatens evil. (p. 252)

Newman does not argue the matter. He just lays it down that conscience is a first principle. Furthermore, he holds that the initial aspect under which a man should meet God is that of the Judge, the reason being that men more frequently fall short of following their conscience than succeed in abiding by it. Further, this Judge has for his governing principle not only mercy, but retributive justice. God does not simply leave sinners to be punished by their own folly, though He does do this; nor does He only punish sinners so that they might be healed, though He does this, too. Rather, He also punishes sinners because they have disturbed a divine balance which can be restored only by the suffering of the offender. For this reason, the notion that unrepentant sinners will suffer for all eternity in an afterlife has a place in the religious scheme of things. Such is Newman's stark view of the information supplied by conscience. Here, he has described his primary informant about the relationship of man to God. This voice has the primacy; it will be the judge of the evidence supplied by the two other informants of natural religion; namely, the voice of mankind and the course of the world.

The Narrow Gate

The voice of conscience, then, is the standard, the narrow gate of the argument. It provides the basic experience which selects and judges from among the other informants of natural and revealed religion. It accepts what agrees with conscience as a sign of God and rejects what offends it as a corruption of evil. Formed in the context of a community, it nevertheless appeals finally to its own judgment. In short, it provides a man, educated or not, with the possibility of having the illative sense in religious matters.

(2) The Voice of Mankind

Let us now consider the second informant about natural religion, the voice of mankind. For his facts, Newman draws upon a book called The Penny Cyclopaedia (p. 253) an account that passed for general knowledge in the educated world of his day. In his selection of the facts, Newman gives much more weight to the testimony of barbaric religions than to those of civilized peoples like the Greeks and Romans. Why? Despite its excesses, primitive religion gives witness to the fear of man before the Judge. They have priests to offer sacrifice in order to intercede for them with God. They enact rites of atonement to make up for past offenses. In contrast, the religion of a civilized people has substituted for the dark intimations of conscience a brighter picture of the gods on Mount Olympus worked into graceful myths by the poets. Newman cites the poet Lucretius as a cultivated man who simply hates the old barbaric religions and chooses the more graceful reign of "Alma Venus".

Not New to Newman

This judgment about civilized societies is not new to Newman. In a sermon given in 1834, he proclaims: "I will not shrink from uttering my firm conviction, that it would be a gain to this country, were it vastly more superstitious, more bigoted, more gloomy, more fierce in its religion, than at present it shows itself to be." As we saw earlier in his sermon "The Infidelity of the Future," the total infidelity will be that of a civilized society which will totally reject traditional religion. This total unbelief is the logical outcome of the civilized man's effort to substitute reason for the voice of conscience. It particularly rejects as an insult to human dignity the notion of eternal punishment in hell.

(3) The Course of the World

When Newman comes to examine the course of the world as the third informant of natural religion, he speaks of the history of the human race. Certainly, there are many different ways in which this history can be interpreted. For example, a secularist, holding that men's brutal behavior to each other is caused by their religion, will see the solution to these evils by getting rid of religion and making way for science. Newman of course differs. His illative sense is guided by one set of principles. The informal and natural reasoning of others is guided by a different set. In the following account of Newman's view, then, we will see how the same historical facts lead to vastly different interpretations.

God's Absence

Newman points out that the man of conscience, holding to the belief that God created man, is appalled by the seeming absence of the Creator from the affairs of men. Though men in the past usually professed some kind of religion, they did not seem to be deterred in the least from the ruthless pursuit of their own ambitions. Most men acted as if there were no God while still professing some kind of belief in the Divine, an instance of secret infidelity. It seems, then, either that there is no God or that he has hidden Himself from His own creation due to some primordial offense committed by man. The believer concludes that the Deity is a Hidden God who does not seem to rule but nevertheless does, a truth known only to those trying to follow their conscience.

Facing the same impression that God is absent from the world, the modern unbeliever will conclude that He is absent because of the simple reason that he does not exist in the first place. He holds, then, that since primitive men could not live as enlightened atheists, they projected upon the world the image of an angry God intent on the punishment of sin. Since, however, modern man can take heart from the progress of science, he no longer needs this projection. The famous "Death of God" proclaimed by Nietzsche has prepared the way for the adulthood of man. Man, then, is not a guilty creature, naturally. Rather, he is a naturally good person who has been made to feel guilty by religious belief.

Suffering

Newman points to the vast amount of suffering in the world in which the innocent suffer as well as the guilty in physical disasters. Further, the just suffer from the unjust in human affairs. Echoing the thoughts of the primitives, he concludes that there must be another powerful but malignant intelligence operating in the world at cross-purposes to the Creator. Consequently, mankind is the battleground on which good and evil, light and darkness engage in a titanic struggle. For the modern unbeliever, however, the existence of the Devil is simply a projection of man's own worst impulses.

Again, Newman notes the fact that there has always been some form of priesthood in the past as a sign of man's desire to atone for his sins through the intercession of someone whom he considered to be holier than himself. Here the special few intercede for the sinful many, attesting to a natural sense of hierarchy in religious matters. In contrast, the modern unbeliever often interprets the fact of priesthood as an expedient devised by the ruling class to maintain its hold over the populace.

Again, Newman notes that in human affairs the few by their

actions bring benefits upon the many. Soldiers die for the fellow citizens, parents sacrifice themselves for their children, and even some heroic rulers lay down their lives that the nation might live. But the few can also bring disaster upon the heads of their dependents. Cowardly soldiers betray their fellow citizens, spendthrift fathers impoverish their descendants, and rulers use their people for their own ambitions. The fact is, then, that human beings are part of a community both for good and for evil. Consequently, primitive men have little difficulty with the notion of intercession in religious matters. Priests can intercede with God to save their people. Modern men, perhaps influenced by the Protestants of the Sixteenth Century who rejected all kinds of intercession, be it that of priests offering sacrifice or of people praying to saints, insist that man stands alone. If one is religious, he deals with God directly, doing away with all mediators. If he is not religious, he takes the pose of being existentially responsible only to himself.

Brighter Side

Again, Newman notes that primitive religious practices have, despite their dark side, a brighter side as well. Otherwise, why would men bother with religion at all if it held no hope for them? They have experience of the bountifulness of nature and of the tranquility of family life. Why should not a man of conscience, then, hope for better things from God who is good? In the light of these same facts, the modern unbeliever might take them as a sign that man has been happy even in the midst of superstition. How much happier, then, would man be if he eliminated the notion of religion altogether and, relying upon his own efforts, constructed utopia with the aid of science? Again, we see how important first principles are when men evaluate the course of the world.

An Admission

If I followed Newman's maxim that egoism is true modesty, I would have to admit that until about fifteen years ago

Newman's discussion of natural religion never registered with me. Even when I sat myself down, determined to grasp his argument by writing outlines of it, I would find the argument going in one ear and out the other. That was until I learned more about natural religion from a Samoan who was one of my students in the seminary. Because he was a Catholic from a nation that had only converted to the faith in the eighteen fifties, I got a fresh picture of what natural religion looks like in the context of a strong community. Religion was not just in the community. Rather, it made the community. God, called Atua in the Samoan language, was the author of the land and of the living creatures in it. From his authority flows the authority invested in the chiefs and tribe, dictating the family structure, ceremonies, and customs. The result was a tough society which had no patience for disobedience on a human or divine level. Samoans are usually quite forceful and decisive for better or worse. For at least over a thousand years, this people on two small islands in the middle of the Pacific Ocean lived upon this belief right up until the middle of the nineteenth century. Then they converted to the Catholic Church, acknowledging that Atua was God the Father who had sent Christ his Son to them. Thus, they effected a union between natural and supernatural religion which is still evident today.

Step of the Argument

Newman has set the intellectual and moral foundations for his search into the truth of the Catholic Church in the traditions of natural religion. At this point, then, there is no longer any great mystery of how the ordinary man can attain true belief about this complex matter. Here a man, though he may be ordinary from the viewpoint of modern education, is extraordinary in this respect; namely, that he has acquired an illative sense within the context of a community which has embodied the best traditions of natural reason. He is an ordinary man looking for a religious answer, a rather extraordinary man after all.

Chapter Fifteen

The Truth of Revelation (Chapter Ten of the *Essay*)

So far, Newman has, after laying down the voice of conscience as his first principle, sorted through the evidence supplied by the history of natural religion, and has listed the expectations the good man has as he searches for a definite revelation from God. Just as men are equipped with the illative sense to discover the right beliefs in their respective fields, so the man who follows his conscience is equipped with an illative sense to discover the truth in the religious field, which is that God has revealed Himself as a baby, youth, and man to mankind.

Before Newman begins his account of this search, however, he reflects upon his method of argument: "In thus speaking of Natural Religion as in one sense a matter of private judgment, and that of proceeding from it to a proof of Christianity, I seem to give up the intention of demonstrating either. Certainly I do; not that I deny that demonstration is possible. Truth certainly, as such, rests upon grounds intrinsically and objectively and abstractedly demonstrative... ." (p. 273) Nevertheless, Newman will stick to his own method of argument, which has been putting together various strands of probable truths to attain the certitude, not of a mathematician, but of a full human being.

The Procedure of Paley

What does Newman have in mind when he speaks of the method of demonstration? It the procedure of Paley as illustrated in the book Evidences for Christianity (p. 273) Newman describes this work as an effort to create a formal or scientific argument which requires very few presumptions on the part of the reader. The author asks only that his readers be open-minded. Hence, he constructs an argument almost mathematical in its precision by drawing especially upon the evidence that miracles play in supporting the case for revelation.

While admitting that there is something that looks like charity in Paley's effort to go out to the highways and byways in order to compel people to come in, Newman nevertheless criticizes this approach. He points out that such arguments operate on the presumption that the reader can approach religious truth in a perfectly detached way with little to hope or fear about the outcome. On the contrary, Newman maintains that a man facing the truth of Christianity is a sinful creature, not a judge sitting comfortably in his armchair coolly weighing the evidence to see whether God has made His case. It is up to man to seek God in fear and trembling, not up to God to meet the canons of rationality set up by armchair philosophers. Newman's goal is to make an argument for a real religion with roots rather than a surface religion based on sheer inference, which is always open for revision when new intellectual trends present themselves.

Another Criticism

Another criticism that Newman levels at this "demonstrative" approach of Paley's is that it prevents an author like himself from using the elements of his personal experience and puts him into the straight jacket of fitting his argument into a quasi-mathematical form. For instance, Paley will concentrate upon compiling an exhaustive account of miracles as if to overwhelm the reader with proof of the supernatural origins of Christianity without taking into account that the reader might have no experience of a miracle in his own life. Newman cries out: "If I am asked to use Paley's argument for my own conversion, I say plainly that I do not want to be converted by a smart syllogism; if I am asked to convert others by it, I say plainly that I do not wish to overcome their reason without touching their hearts. I wish to deal, not with controversialists, but with inquirers." (p. 273)

Antecedent Probability

Let us now consider a few other observations which Newman makes upon his method of argument. He acknowledges that, after he has framed the beginning of his argument in the context of natural religion, he has gone a long way towards making his case. A man of conscience has the strong antecedent presumption that God will reveal himself in a special way. So, when he reflects upon his own experience and looks out upon the world, he weighs these events with the hope that he will find a special revelation from God. Thus, what may look like a violent improbability to an indifferent man will seem more probable to him. Why should a man who stumbles over the truth that God exists ever look for any special revelation from God? Why should a man who is satisfied with himself be looking to change his heart? He is quite content with himself as he sits upon the heads of other men, considering his position as the natural order of things. But the man looking to change his heart will be predisposed to look out upon the world for any signs that God has revealed Himself to save him from his own pride.

Little Positive Evidence

Newman gives an example of just how strongly this personal sense of antecedent probability works.

> ...very little positive evidence seems to be necessary, when the mind is penetrated by the strong anticipation which I am supposing. It was this instinctive apprehension, as we may conjecture, which carried on

> Dionysus and Damaris at Athens to a belief in Christianity, though St. Paul did no miracle there, and only asserted the doctrines of the Divine Unity, the Resurrection, and the universal judgment, while, on the other hand, it had no tendency to attach them to any of the mythological rites in which the place abounded. (p.273)

Some might accuse these two listeners of St. Paul as being so credulous that they were ready to believe in anything. But there were many beliefs in Athens which they might have swallowed if they were so credulous. Then why did they believe St. Paul? Might it not have been that they saw the convergence of three distinct religious teachings in the preaching of one man as a sign of the truth? The teachings of the Unity of God and the universal judgment were not new to a Greek listener. But the teaching of the Resurrection in which men were to be reunited with their bodies was new and indeed repulsed many of St. Paul's listeners--but not Dionysius and Damarius. Now these two, apparently the type of Greeks who hung around the public forum listening to philosophical discourses of every description, had been raised upon the same beliefs of credence that their fellow citizens had. Why did they not reject the resurrection of the dead as the others had? Newman conjectures that they converted because they had real belief in the existence of God as a reality and so were able to see the convergence of probabilities in the words of St. Paul. Others saw only an improbable tale told by a wandering Jew.

Who was being more rational? Believers hold that the pair reasoned correctly and the others were wrong. What constitutes the proper use of reason looks like irrationality to the world. Again, we see the operations of first principles under the heading of antecedent presumptions. Logically, presumptions about what is probable cannot themselves prove a fact. But they do determine the attitude of the man who looks out into the world for indications of the fact in question. If he judges that enough of these probabilities converge towards the truth he is seeking, he attains belief.

Though St. Paul worked no miracles, the two Athenians saw St. Paul as a messenger from God.

Newman Begins His Argument

Let's now consider Newman's argument for the truth of Christianity. He observes that if Christianity is not the fulfillment of the expectations of conscience, then God has not yet revealed Himself to man. This is a very strong claim. He goes on to deny that he is speaking as one who has not only been brought up a Christian but also as one who has taken into account the outline of natural religion. I believe many Catholics would hesitate to take such a stand because, having been raised in the Church, they cannot easily distinguish between the natural and the supernatural order. Their notions of conscience, of natural religion, of the Old and the New Testaments, of the teachings of the Church, are all mixed together so that they cannot sort out the elements that belong to reason alone and those which belong to faith, the result being that they are uncertain about how to proceed in a strictly philosophical argument. Newman intends to lead the way in this matter.

A Priesthood

He has already shown that a dominant feature of natural religion is the institution of a priesthood offering sacrifice as a mediator between God and man. This institution is communal. Since it is subject to many corruptions, as can be seen in the practice of human sacrifice and of the religions of the classical period, the good man has nevertheless the expectation that God will reveal himself more directly. Though Newman does not bring up this specific point here, I have interjected it because it very forcibly dramatizes the claim that, if one considers all the religions in the world today, he will see that Christianity, specifically the Catholic Church, is the one religion which has a priesthood interceding for the whole world by offering the unbloody sacrifice of the Mass.

The point that Newman does bring up in this section is the ethical continuity between the heathen moralists and the Fathers of the Church. Since the Fathers were close to the fact of paganism, they had a clear idea of the strengths and weaknesses of natural religion so that they would be able to see how the supernatural religion of Christianity completes and perfects it. Thinkers without intimate acquaintance with natural religion are not able to argue in this way. At any rate, Newman specifically mentions here Aristotle among the pagan moralists, whom he acknowledges as his secular master. (p. 277)

The History of the Jews

Newman then takes up the history of the Jews because one cannot speak intelligently about Christianity without speaking of them. As Hilaire Belloc once said: How odd of God to choose the Jews. Christianity claims that it arose from and was first preached by members of the Jewish nation. Now, the noteworthy thing was that the Jews, alone among ancient peoples, had preserved the belief in the One God when all others had descended into polytheism. From the very beginning of their history, the Jews recounted in their sacred books how their natural belief was confirmed by an explicit revelation from God that He and no other was the One God. Further, their records tell of how God promised Abraham that he would be the Father of a people who would bring blessings to the whole world. Newman emphasizes this feature of a universal benefit to all of mankind as being unique. Other nations took for granted that each had their own gods who would look after them. While the Jews considered themselves as specially chosen, they nevertheless had the teaching that God, being Creator of all peoples, had a plan for all peoples. Further, they also had the expectation, which had been instilled in them by the prophets, that the plan of God would be fulfilled through the coming of a Messiah who would be of their own flesh and blood. It was through the coming of this Messiah that all nations would be blessed.

The Records

The records of both the Jews and of the pagans show that at the time of Christ the Jews expected the coming of the long-awaited Messiah. To verify the fact, Newman quotes several Roman historians, one of whom I will present here. "A persuasion had possession of most of them" says Tacitus, speaking of their resistance to the Romans, "that it was contained in the ancient books of the priests, that at the very time the East should prevail, and that men who should issue from Judea should obtain the Empire. The common people, as is the way with human cupidity, having once interpreted in their own favor this grand destiny, were not even by their reverses brought round to the truth of facts." History also shows that Christ, who announced Himself as the Messiah, was rejected by many of the Jewish people. Though this people alone had preserved the belief in One God for two thousand years, they had expected a Messiah who as a conqueror would restore the Kingdom of Israel before the eyes of the world. Instead, Christ came preaching of a kingdom that was not of this world. The Jewish leaders crucified him as a blasphemer though it was the Apostles, all Jewish, who accepted the crucified Christ as the savior of the whole world. About forty years later, the Romans destroyed the Temple and scattered the Jewish people to all ends of the earth where they have somehow survived from that day to this as a people without a nation.

The Point

The objection could be raised that the history of the Jews shows how a people could be misled in their belief in God. But not all were misled, the Apostles and the Jewish Christians being an exception. For those who were misled, their history shows that the promise of God hinged upon the condition that the Jewish people would be faithful to their covenant with God. Since a man of conscience realizes that man has free will, he knows that his rejection is quite possible if he fails to choose properly. At the same time, he also knows that, if he believes properly, he will fulfill the prophecy that salvation will come to the whole earth through the story of the Jewish people.

Subsequent History

The history books show that in about three centuries the Jewish followers of Christ dispersed over the known world, converting the Gentiles to belief in their Master. The promise given to Abraham was fulfilled. The Roman Empire, which had done all that it could to resist this new religion, became officially Christian in 313 with the coming of Constantine. Newman does not mention this last point because his argument is intent on portraying preceding rapid spread of Christianity in its three centuries of struggle against the Empire. The rapid spread of Christianity is such a gigantic phenomenon that even an atheistic historian like Gibbon, the author of the famous work *The Decline and Fall of the Roman Empire*, had to attempt an explanation. An historical fact is, after all, a fact no matter how people interpret it. Newman reviews the explanation, points out its inadequacy, and then suggests the reason why this great writer was incapable of dealing properly with this subject. In giving his reasons for the spread of Christianity, Gibbon never seriously considered the account supplied by the Christians themselves. The Christians explained their success in the fact that they preached a Christ who was not only crucified but was God himself. How could an atheist enter into this kind of a religious explanation for the spread of Christianity?

Two Things

To explain the spread of Christianity, Newman does two things. He shows from the accounts of the early Christians themselves that the principle of their conversion and of their fellowship was the Image of Christ working within them. And he will show that the success of this fellowship took place mainly in the lower classes, who had no power, influence, reputation, or education. Again, we have reference to community, which functions according to the notional beliefs of credence and the real beliefs of assent. Concerning the first point, Newman cites the words of the Apostles and St. Paul to the effect that their message is about the crucified Christ. They all proclaim that it is the Image or Thought of the Crucified which worked a moral conversion in themselves and provided the basis for their fellowship. Now an inquirer can either accept or reject this testimony. But the testimony is there. Seeing how Newman uses this testimony in his argument, we can see why he so carefully laid down in previous chapters the distinction between notional and real assent. Notional assent is given to the truth of a proposition. Real assent is given to a Reality which impresses itself upon a man as a living Image. Newman is intent to show, then, that as a matter of fact real apprehension was at work in the preaching and acceptance of that Image by the early Christians.

Second Point

Newman then goes on to elaborate on his second point, namely, that it was largely the poor and the dispossessed who took this Image to their hearts. Here again is a community or class which tends to have a very different view of life than their betters. Newman devotes many pages recording the historical testimony of those who were converted to the Image as well as those who despised it. He cites the testimony of pagan authors, who characterized the members of the new religion as weak-minded and uneducated. These well-educated officials simply could not understand what has gotten into those people who would undergo unspeakable torments rather than go through the formality of giving homage to the Emperor and denying their Christ. Newman goes on to relate accounts of the martyrs from the Christian records, telling story after story about ordinary men and women, the young and the old maintaining their faith amid grisly torments. They accept all the tortures that the ingenuity of an outraged Empire can devise in order to preserve its own idea of order. Finally, the Empire gives way in exhaustion, the persecutors more weary of slaughtering than their victims of being slaughtered. Here is an indication that the common people can attain real belief with certitude even in the face of unspeakable suffering.

The Explanation of the Christians

What Newman has done is to take the historical fact that Christianity did triumph over Imperial Rome and then to record the Christians' own explanation for this triumph. What judgment will the inquirer make on this testimony? If he is skeptical, he need not accept this testimony, arguing that a solely religious motivation cannot be powerful enough to explain a social revolution. He may look for an economic interpretation like the Marxists. Or he may attribute the success of Christianity to the fanatical spirit that seems to dominate the masses in certain periods of history as in the spread of the Islam shows. In any case each inquirer will have to wrestle with the fact that Christianity did spread with amazing rapidity. His explanation of the fact will be determined by his own first principles.

Not Miracles

Some Christian apologists place a great deal of stress upon the miracles that attended the story of Christ. Newman is certainly not opposed to the truth of these miracles and indeed spent a great deal of effort in other works to defending the reality of miracles. But in his argument he is looking for a more personal way to provide the evidence for the reality of the supernatural. He has one in the fact that Christ did not come down from the cross, a miracle that surely would have impressed everyone there. Yet a thief suffering for his sins on a cross performs the super human act of seeing in the innocence of a fellow suffering the face of God. That is the kind of miracle that Newman wishes to note.

The Last Section

In the last section of his book, Newman makes a grand summary. I will cite a large section of it to show how he as philosopher looks back upon his effort:

> I have been forestalling all along the thought with which

The Truth of Revelation

I shall close these considerations on the subject of Christianity; and necessarily forestalling it, because it properly comes first, though the course which my argument has taken has not allowed me to introduce it in its natural place. *Revelation begins where Natural Religion fails.* [my italics] The Religion of Nature is a mere inchoation, and needs a complement,--it can have but one complement, and that very complement is Christianity. Natural religion is based upon the sense of sin; it recognizes the disease, but it cannot find, it does but look out for the remedy. That remedy, both for guilt and moral impotence, is found in the central doctrine of Revelation, the Mediation of Christ. ... Thus it is that Christianity is the fulfillment made to Abraham, and of the Mosaic revelation; this is how it has been able from the first to occupy the world and gain a hold on every class of human society to which its preachers reached; this is why the Roman power and the multitude of religions which it embraced could not stand against it; this is the secret of its sustained energy, and its never-flagging martyrdoms; this is how at present it is so mysteriously potent, in spite of the new and fearful adversaries which beset its path. *It has with it that gift of staunching and healing the one deep wound of human nature,* [my italics] which avails more for its success than a full encyclopedia of scientific knowledge and a whole library of controversy, and therefore it must last while human nature lasts. It is a living truth which never can grow old. (p. 313)

Newman follows this declaration with a more specific description of how the Catholic Church deals with the wounds of mankind. First, it has a priesthood which reenacts Christ's death upon the cross everyday throughout the world in the Sacrifice of the Mass. Next, there is in the Eucharist, the entrance of God himself, body, soul and divinity, into the body and soul of believers who have more intimate contact with Christ here and now than those who actually saw Christ in his sojourn upon earth. Next, there is the Real Presence of

Christ in churches throughout the world. The expectation of religious men and women that God would reveal himself in a special way has been fulfilled beyond anything they might have expected.

Conclusion

Perhaps the best way to conclude is to note the next to last paragraph.

> Here I end my specimens, among the many which might be given, of the arguments adducible for Christianity. I have dwelt upon them, in order to show how I would apply the principles of this *Essay* to the proof of its divine origin. *Christianity is addressed, both as regards its evidences and its contents, to minds which are in the normal condition of human nature, as believing in God and in a future judgment.* [italics mine]. Such minds it addresses both through the intellect and through the imagination; creating a certitude of its truth by arguments too various for direct enumeration, too personal and deep for words, too powerful and concurrent for refutation. Nor need reason come first and faith second (though this is the logical order), but one and the same teaching is in different aspects both object and proof, and elicits one complex act of both inference and assent. It speaks to us one by one, and is received by us one by one, as the counterpart, so to say, of ourselves, and is as real as we are real. (p. 315)

It is important to note that all along Newman has been dealing with the natural type of assent that reason is capable of giving to the truth of the Church. Here, reason includes conscience, thus making man naturally religious and putting him in the condition which Newman regards as normal. Yes, he says that the normal or natural condition of man is to believe in God and in future judgment. Some may be shocked at it. Though he may be used to accepting the general teaching of the Church that human reason is capable of belief in the One God without the aid of revelation, he may not have realized that human reason itself was such a powerful instrument. This is what an American Catholic has to realize. He has to renew his confidence in reason again because it provides the natural foundations for supernatural belief. Cut out the foundations and the Church is merely a thing of the past offering a remedy which men no longer need because they are no longer sinners. Put in the foundations and the Church is a two-winged creature which flies up to heaven and back to earth again, a real thing in a real world that carries mankind with it.

This view of full-bodied reason in no way undermines the teaching of the Church that the assent to the truths of supernatural faith is solely a gift of God. By reason alone, man is not capable of giving this kind of assent. God Himself has to supply both the content of faith (otherwise, man could not know of the existence of the Holy Trinity) and the grace to accept it. Thus, it is one thing to assent to the truth of the Church by reason alone and quite another to assent to these truths because of supernatural grace. This is why the Church has always insisted that human reason itself establishes the preambles upon which supernatural faith arises. Without the presumption that there is One God who will judge sinners in the afterlife, there is no reason why men should look for a refuge in the Church. Once a person believes that there is One God, he can then be prompted by grace to make the act of faith, which states that he believes in the teachings of the Church BECAUSE God has revealed them. If he has no real or personal sense that there is a God, a conviction given to him by conscience, how can he see God as the guarantee for the truth of the Church? He will only see the Church as a collection of sinful human beings (which she is) without seeing that God in his mysterious ways has given to those human beings the duty of speaking and acting in his name.

It is upon this view of the matter that Pope John Paul II has written his encyclical *Faith and Reason*. He has included reason in this couplet because it is truly a wing complementing the wing of supernatural faith. The great danger for modern man is the collapse of his reason, as paradoxical as that may seem. In denaturing himself, he becomes incapable, not only of recognizing the Church for what she is, but even of acting like a human being. He then becomes a deadly menace to himself, an enemy of the human dignity he professes in his proclamations but degrades in his practice. So, the Pope and Newman aim at man's reasserting human dignity by respecting reason. In these efforts, they may seem to some like Don Quixote tilting against windmills. There is truth to this. How will an encyclical like the Pope's or a book like Newman's give back to men their reason? Nevertheless, these Captains send out their challenge to good Christian men and women to take up the fight which they always seem to lose, just as Christ seemed to lose when he died on the cross.

The End of the Book

In our investigation of belief, we began with a sermon from Newman. This is the way he ends:

> In the sacred words of its Divine Author and Object concerning Himself, 'I am the Good Shepherd, and I know Mine and Mine know Me. My sheep hear my voice, and I know them, and they follow me. And I give them everlasting life, and they shall never perish, and no man should pluck them out of my hand. (p.316)

The Church is Christ the Good Shepherd leading his flock. Yet, the Good Shepherd sees a division in mankind which, though he came to mend it, will persist to the end of the time and beyond. There will always be this terrible difference among men--they will have to choose between fidelity and infidelity. Perhaps this sobering picture is the reason why Pope John Paul II always closes his encyclicals with a prayer to Mary, the Mother of God. Apocalyptic cataclysms are frightening, sending the thoughts of brave men and women up to Mary as if they were children again running back to their mother. It is a Catholic habit. So, I ask her in the words of the Hail Mary to "pray for us sinners, now and at the hour of our death. Amen."

Afterword

Having completed the argument of Part II entitled "Assent and Inference," I have been tempted to write a summary of the steps of the argument. But I have resisted the temptation, feeling that I was getting a bit obsessive in trying to hold on to all the details of the argument both for myself and for you my readers. As best I could, I have already put down all the steps so that following them might be more like mounting a grand staircase than stepping from rock to rock in a raging stream. But, it is now time to let my case rest. At this point in my life, my brain is not as retentive as it used to be. I have difficulty in remembering where I put my damned cane, let alone recalling all the steps Newman has taken in constructing his argument. Instead, I find myself taking great pleasure in going through the questions and answers of the Baltimore Catechism. The Church asks the question and then supplies the answer. I just have to ride along. Similarly, I am learning how to say the Rosary. For many years I said mystery after mystery, decade after decade, a much less exciting trip than following philosophical arguments. But now I am content just to go along with the flow. The angel tells Mary she is to be the Mother of God. Then she goes to visit her cousin Elizabeth. And then the Baby is born in a stable attended by the mother and father, a few shepherds, three Kings, donkeys and sheep about, and angels singing overhead. It's quite a picture.

Occasionally, I recall some forgotten events in my own life. As I get older, I sometimes find myself sitting still for fifteen minutes at a time without being able to recall what I was thinking about. Then I snap out of it and open the fridge or wash a dish. It's all quite mellow! There's something to be said for a sheep placidly grazing on the grass as the Good Shepherd keeps watch. But since there is still some fight left in me, I check the INTERNET and see what Church Militant is up to.

It is a group composed of good sheep. But they are fighting sheep in the vigor of their youth. The details of their argument are important to remember because they have come on the stage of life at a time when younger generations are truly lost sheep being swallowed up by an apocalypse. They are in great need of hearing the Good News and then rallying around the standard showing that the Devil and his cohorts do not run the world. The Lamb of God does, the King who allowed Himself to be crucified in order to point out that the Kingdom of God comes in final glory in the next life, not this one.

www.ingramcontent.com/pod-product-compliance
Lightning Source LLC
Chambersburg PA
CBHW032125160426

43197CB00008B/527